Sunset

Holiday
COOK BOOK

Recipes in this book were previously published
as part of the Sunset *book* Christmas Treasury

By the Editors of Sunset Books
and Sunset Magazine

Spread holiday cheer with gaily decorated gifts of homemade sweet
breads. Shown here (clockwise from front) are Swedish Kardemum-
makrans (page 31), Cranberry-Nut Bread (page 29) baked in two
different sizes, Dresden-style Stollen (page 38), and Cherry-Almond
Christmas Wreath (page 78) shaped like a candy cane.

Lane Publishing Co. ■ Menlo Park, California

Happy Holidays!

Beginning with Thanksgiving celebrations and progressing right through the festive Christmas season, food and drink express the expansive good spirits of the holidays. Whether you're looking for delectable cookie recipes for Christmas gift-giving or a complete menu for a sumptuous holiday open house, you'll find ideas galore in this book.

In the first chapter, we offer a wealth of recipes for cookies, breads, cakes, pies, and candies—both to give as gifts and to serve to your guests and family.

For all your holiday entertaining, look in the second chapter—you'll discover a menu for every occasion, from Thanksgiving dinner to Christmas breakfast. We've given you twelve menus in all, including beverage suggestions and recipes.

Finally, for a selection of spectacular Christmas Day dinners, turn to the last chapter. Our menus feature a mouthwatering array of centerpiece roasts, ranging from golden goose to succulent beef, with all the trimmings.

Whether your holidays are a time for lavish entertaining or cozy family gatherings, elaborate baking or quick and easy cooking, you're sure to find ideas and inspiration right here. So put on your apron and start cooking!

For their expert advice on menus and recipes, we'd like to thank Joan Griffiths and Sue Brownlee. Special thanks also go to JoAnn Masaoka, Lynne B. Morrall, and Karen Hazarian for styling some of the photos, and to Kathy Barone for laying out the individual book pages.

About the Recipes

All of the recipes in this book were tested and developed in the *Sunset* test kitchens.

Home Economics Editor, Sunset Magazine

Jerry Anne Di Vecchio

Book Editor

Cynthia Overbeck Bix

Coordinating Editor

Suzanne Normand Mathison

Contributing Editor

Rebecca LaBrum

Design

Sandra Popovich

Photography

Glenn Christiansen: 10, 33, 34, 49. **Kris Knutson:** 61, 65, 80, 83, 91. **Michael Lamotte:** 66. **Stephen Marley:** 42, 56, 79, 86. **Norman A. Plate:** 69, 94. **David Stubbs:** 7. **Darrow M. Watt:** 2, 4, 15, 18, 23, 26, 39, 46, 58. **Tom Wyatt:** 1, 29, 53, 73, 75.

Editor, Sunset Books: Elizabeth L. Hogan

Second printing July 1989

Cover: A festive holiday table welcomes guests to our sumptuous Roast Beef Dinner (pages 90–91). Occupying center stage is a juicy tangerine-glazed roast. Prosciutto appetizers, Swiss chard, and rich corn risotto round out the menu. Cover design by Carol Hatchard Goforth. Photography by Glenn Christiansen. Food styling by Paula Smith Freschet.

Topped with sweetened sour cream and crunchy walnuts, Creamy Pumpkin Pie Squares (page 48) make a delightful alternative to traditional pumpkin pie for a holiday feast.

Contents

4

Baked Goods & Confections

■

Hand-molded & Pressed Cookies
Cutout Cookies
Drop Cookies
Bar Cookies
Icebox Cookies
Quick Breads
Yeast Breads
Cakes
Pies & Tarts
Candies

56

Festive Holiday Menus

■

Easy Thanksgiving Banquet
Tree-cutters' Tailgate Picnic
Tree-trimmers' Buffet Supper
Holiday Open House
Expandable Buffet Party
Easy-going Holiday Suppers
Children's Christmas Party
Festive Dessert Buffet
Christmas Eve Family Supper
Christmas Morning Breakfast

80

Christmas Day Feasts

■

Roast Turkey Dinner
Roast Goose Dinner
Roast Pork Dinner
Roast Beef Dinner
Make-ahead Christmas Dinner

95

Index

■

Special Features

Packaging & Sending Cookies   9
Holiday Potluck Supper   70
New Year's Day Breakfast   94

Baked Goods & Confections

From Thanksgiving pies to Christmas cookies to the sweet Golden Teddy Bear Breads (page 30) shown below, the goodies you make for the holidays express the generous and joyous spirit of the season. In this chapter, you'll find a wonderful collection of delectable recipes for holiday giving and for enjoying at home.

Hand-molded & Pressed Cookies

Using your hands and a few simple tools, you can create an array of fancy Christmas cookies fit for a pastry shop window. For Spritz—a holiday classic—you'll need a cookie press; just by changing the plates, you can make wreaths, trees, starbursts, and any number of other shapes. But our other cookies—crumbly-rich Almond Crescents, nut-crusted Thumbprint Cookies, and more— are all easily shaped by hand.

Almond Crescents
(Pictured on page 75)

A snowy mantle of powdered sugar cloaks these buttery, brandy-spiked nut cookies. Called *kourabiedes,* they're a Greek specialty—perfect for a yuletide cookie tray, or for teatime in any season.

- ½ cup ground almonds
- 1 cup (½ lb.) unsalted butter or margarine, at room temperature
- 1 large egg yolk
- 2 tablespoons powdered sugar
- 1 tablespoon brandy or ½ teaspoon vanilla
- 2 cups all-purpose flour
- ½ teaspoon baking powder Whole cloves (optional)
- 1½ to 2 cups powdered sugar

Spread almonds in a shallow baking pan and toast in a 350° oven until lightly browned (6 to 8 minutes), shaking pan occasionally. Let cool completely.

In large bowl of an electric mixer, beat butter until creamy. Add egg yolk and the 2 tablespoons sugar, mixing well. Stir in brandy and almonds. In another bowl, stir together flour and baking powder. Gradually add to butter mixture, blending thoroughly.

Pinch off dough in 1-inch balls and roll each into a 2- to 2½-inch rope. Place ropes about 2 inches apart on ungreased baking sheets; shape into crescents. Insert a whole clove in each crescent, if desired. Bake in a 325° oven until very lightly browned (about 30 minutes). Place baking sheets on racks and let cookies cool for 5 minutes.

Sift about half the 1½ to 2 cups sugar over a sheet of wax paper. Transfer cookies to paper, placing them in a single layer. Sift remaining sugar over cookies to cover. Let stand until cool. Store airtight; remove clove (if used) from each cookie before eating. Makes about 2½ dozen.

Anise Pretzels
(Pictured on page 15)

The attractive shape of these anise-flavored cookies makes them a good choice for gifts, parties, or hanging on the tree. The anise flavor may remind you of *springerle,* an old-fashioned German cookie—and if you wish, you can shape the dough as you would for springerle, using the traditional carved rolling pin to produce little square cookies with embossed patterns.

- 1 cup (½ lb.) butter or margarine, at room temperature
- ½ cup sugar
- 2 large eggs
- 1½ teaspoons anise extract
- 3½ cups all-purpose flour
- 1 large egg beaten with 1 tablespoon water (omit if shaping dough with a springerle rolling pin)
- 1 to 2 tablespoons anise seeds

In large bowl of an electric mixer, beat butter and sugar until creamy; beat in the 2 eggs, 1 at a time, beating until well combined after each addition. Beat in anise extract. Gradually add flour, blending thoroughly.

Divide dough in half. For pretzels, roll each half into a log 2 inches in diameter. For picture cookies, shape each half into a rectangular slab. Wrap tightly in plastic wrap and refrigerate until easy to handle (at least 1 hour).

For pretzels: Cut logs of dough into ⅜-inch-thick slices. Roll each slice into a rope about 14 inches long, then twist into a pretzel shape. Place on greased baking sheets, spacing at least 1 inch apart. Brush with egg-water mixture, then sprinkle lightly with anise seeds. Bake in a 325° oven until light golden and firm to the touch (about 20 minutes). Transfer to racks and let cool. Store airtight. Makes about 2 dozen.

For picture cookies: On a lightly floured board, roll out dough, half at a time, to form a ¼-inch-thick rectangle slightly wider than your springerle rolling pin. Pressing down firmly, roll springerle rolling pin once over dough so that designs are sharply imprinted. With a sharp knife, cut pictures into squares, following lines made by springerle rolling pin.

Sprinkle each of 2 greased baking sheets with about 1 tablespoon anise seeds. Set cookies about 1 inch apart on seeds. Bake in a 325° oven until bottoms are golden and tops are firm to the touch but still white (15 to 18 minutes). Transfer to racks and let cool. Store airtight. Makes about 3½ dozen.

Speculaas

In Dutch homes, cookies are baked in profusion for *Sinterklaas avond* (the eve of St. Nicholas Day). Perhaps the best known of these holiday treats are crisp and spicy *speculaas*, traditionally shaped by pressing the dough into elaborately carved wooden molds. If you have a speculaas mold (they're sometimes sold in cookware shops), you'll be able to make cookies with old-fashioned embossed designs; if you don't, you can just roll out the dough and cut it with your favorite cookie cutters.

> 2   cups all-purpose flour
> 2   teaspoons ground cinnamon
> ½   teaspoon **each** baking powder and ground nutmeg
> 1   teaspoon ground cloves
> ⅛   teaspoon salt
> ¼   cup ground blanched almonds
> 1   cup firmly packed brown sugar
> ¾   cup (⅜ lb.) firm butter or margarine, cut into pieces
> 2   tablespoons milk

In a large bowl, stir together flour, cinnamon, baking powder, nutmeg, cloves, and salt. Blend in almonds and sugar until well combined. With a pastry blender or 2 knives, cut in butter until mixture resembles cornmeal; stir in milk. Work dough with your hands until you can form it into a smooth ball.

For molded cookies: Press dough firmly and evenly into a floured wooden speculaas mold; invert onto an ungreased baking sheet and release cookie by tapping back of mold (ease cookies out with the point of a knife, if necessary). Space cookies about 1 inch apart.

For rolled cookies: On a lightly floured board, roll out dough to a thickness of about ¼ inch. Cut out with 2- to 3-inch cookie cutters. Transfer to ungreased baking sheets, spacing cookies about 1 inch apart.

Bake molded or rolled cookies in a 300° oven until lightly browned (20 to 25 minutes). Let cool briefly on baking sheets; transfer to racks and let cool completely. Store airtight. Makes about 4 dozen.

Crisp Oatmeal Fruit Strips
(Pictured on facing page)

Here's a big batch of cookies you can make in a hurry. You shape the dough into long logs, then cut each log into strips after baking. Use your choice of raisins, prunes, or dates in the dough—or try some of each.

> 1   cup (½ lb.) butter or margarine, at room temperature
> 1½   cups sugar
> 1   large egg
> 2   cups all-purpose flour
> 2   teaspoons baking soda
> 2   cups raisins, finely diced pitted prunes, or finely snipped pitted dates
> 1¼   cups rolled oats

In large bowl of an electric mixer, beat butter and sugar until fluffy. Beat in egg. In another bowl, stir together flour and baking soda; stir into creamed mixture along with raisins and oats.

Divide dough into 15 equal portions. Place 3 or 4 portions on each ungreased 12- by 15-inch baking sheet; pinch and press each dough portion to make an 8-inch-long rope. Position ropes at least 2 inches apart on baking sheets; flatten each rope to make a 2-inch-wide strip.

Bake in a 350° oven until golden brown (about 10 minutes). Let cool on baking sheets for about 2 minutes, then cut each strip diagonally into 1-inch-wide bars. Let cookies cool on baking sheets. Store airtight. Makes about 12 dozen.

Twice-baked Walnut Cookies
(Pictured on facing page)

Toasted to a golden crunch, these anise-accented nut cookies are delightful with coffee or tea. They mail well, too.

> 4   eggs
> 1½   cups sugar
> ¾   cup (⅜ lb.) butter or margarine, melted
> 2   teaspoons vanilla
> 1   teaspoon **each** anise extract and black walnut flavoring
> ½   teaspoon almond extract
> 1   cup chopped walnuts
> 5   cups all-purpose flour
> 4½   teaspoons baking powder

In a large bowl, beat together eggs and sugar with a heavy spoon until well blended. Stir in butter, vanilla, anise extract, black walnut flavoring, almond extract, and walnuts.

In another bowl, stir together flour and baking powder. Gradually stir into creamed mixture, blending well.

On a floured board, divide dough into 8 equal portions. Roll each into a 14-inch rope. Place ropes about 2 inches apart on greased 12- by 15-inch baking sheets.

Bake in a 325° oven until bottoms of ropes are pale gold (about 20 minutes). Let cool for about 2 minutes on baking sheets, then cut each rope diagonally into ½- to ¾-inch-thick slices.

Tip slices onto cut sides; lay close together on baking sheets. Bake in a 375° oven until lightly toasted (about 15 more minutes). Let cool on sheets. Store airtight. Makes about 12 dozen.

Bake up big batches of delectable Twice-baked Walnut Cookies and Crisp Oatmeal Fruit Strips (facing page) and Almond Ravioli Cookies (page 17) in no time, using quick "assembly-line" techniques.

Brandy Balls

The flavor of brandy enlivens these rich holiday nuggets. They're much like Almond Crescents (page 5), but filled with pecans instead of almonds —and rolled into balls, not curved into crescents.

1¼ cups (⅝ lb.) butter or margarine, at room temperature

½ cup granulated sugar
1 large egg yolk
2 teaspoons brandy flavoring
3 cups all-purpose flour
¼ teaspoon salt
1 cup finely chopped pecans or walnuts
  Powdered sugar

In large bowl of an electric mixer, beat butter and granulated sugar until creamy; beat in egg yolk and brandy flavoring. In another bowl, stir together flour and salt; gradually add to butter mixture, blending thoroughly. Stir in pecans until well combined.

Roll dough into 1-inch balls and place about 1 inch apart on lightly greased baking sheets. Bake in a 350° oven until firm to the touch and very light golden (about 25 minutes). Transfer to racks and let cool slightly; while still warm, roll in powdered sugar to coat. Let cool completely. Store airtight. Makes about 4 dozen.

Spritz

(Pictured on page 75)

Buttery, almond-flavored Swedish spritz are always a favorite at holiday time. You can make them in a variety of fancy shapes (depending on which design plate you insert in your cookie press) and dress them up with candied fruit, colored sugar, silver dragées, or other decorations.

> 1   cup (½ lb.) butter, at
>   room temperature
> ¾   cup sugar
> 2   large egg yolks
> 1   teaspoon vanilla
> ½   teaspoon almond extract
> 2½ cups all-purpose flour
> ½   teaspoon baking powder
> ⅛   teaspoon salt
>   Decorations
>   (suggestions follow)

In large bowl of an electric mixer, beat butter until creamy. Gradually add sugar, beating until fluffy. Add egg yolks, 1 at a time, and beat until smooth. Beat in vanilla and almond extract. In another bowl, stir together flour, baking powder, and salt; gradually add to butter mixture, blending thoroughly.

Place dough in a cookie press fitted with a design plate, packing it in firmly and evenly. Force out onto ungreased baking sheets, spacing cookies about 1 inch apart. If kitchen is very warm and dough is soft and sticky, refrigerate until firm enough to press easily. Decorate as desired.

Bake in a 350° oven until edges are lightly browned (12 to 15 minutes). Transfer to racks and let cool. Store airtight. Makes about 4 dozen.

Decorations. Before baking, top cookies with halved **candied cherries**; or sprinkle with finely chopped **nuts**, **colored decorating sugar**, **nonpareils**, **silver dragées**, or **chocolate sprinkles**. Or brush baked cookies with this chocolate glaze: in top of a double boiler over simmering water, melt together 4 ounces **semisweet chocolate** and ½ teaspoon **solid vegetable shortening**. Apply with a pastry brush. Refrigerate glazed cookies for 10 minutes to harden glaze.

Thumbprint Cookies

A sweet "jewel" of jelly sparkles in the center of each of these nutty drop cookies. It rests in a small indentation made by your thumb—or the tip of a spoon, if you prefer.

> 1   cup (½ lb.) butter or
>   margarine, at room
>   temperature
> ½   cup firmly packed
>   brown sugar
> 2   large eggs, separated
> ½   teaspoon vanilla
> 2½ cups all-purpose flour
> ¼   teaspoon salt
> 1½ cups finely chopped
>   walnuts
> 3   to 4 tablespoons red
>   currant jelly or
>   raspberry jam

In large bowl of an electric mixer, beat butter and sugar until creamy. Beat in egg yolks and vanilla. In another bowl, stir together flour and salt. Gradually add to butter mixture, blending thoroughly.

In a small bowl, lightly beat egg whites. With your hands, roll dough into balls about 1 inch in diameter. Dip each ball in egg whites, then roll in walnuts to coat. Place 1 inch apart on greased baking sheets.

With your thumb or the tip of a spoon, make an indentation in center of each ball. Neatly fill each indentation with about ¼ teaspoon jelly.

Bake in a 375° oven until lightly browned (12 to 15 minutes). Let cool on baking sheets for about a minute, then transfer to racks and let cool completely. Store airtight. Makes about 3½ dozen.

Candy Cane Crisps

The month of December is punctuated with occasions calling for cookies, and these crisp morsels suit the season perfectly.

> 1   cup (½ lb.) butter or
>   margarine, at room
>   temperature
>   About 1¼ cups
>   powdered sugar
> 1½ teaspoons vanilla
> 1⅓ cups all-purpose flour
> 1   cup rolled oats
> ½   teaspoon salt
>   About ¾ cup coarsely
>   crushed candy canes or
>   hard peppermint candy

In large bowl of an electric mixer, beat butter and 1 cup of the sugar until creamy; beat in vanilla. In another bowl, stir together flour, oats, and salt; gradually add to butter mixture, blending thoroughly. Add ¼ cup of the crushed candy canes and mix until well combined.

Roll dough into ¾-inch balls, then roll in remaining sugar (about ¼ cup) to coat. Place balls about 2 inches apart on greased and flour-dusted baking sheets. Flatten cookies with a fork, making a crisscross pattern with fork tines. Sprinkle each with about ½ teaspoon crushed candy canes.

Bake in a 325° oven until edges are lightly browned (18 to 20 minutes). Let cool on baking sheets for 2 to 3 minutes, then transfer to racks and let cool completely. Store airtight. Makes about 4 dozen.

Packaging & Sending Cookies

■

Sending homemade cookies to friends and loved ones in faraway places is a Christmas tradition in many families. Here's how to insure a safe arrival for your gifts.

Which cookies to send

Make sure you select cookies that are good travelers. They must be sturdy enough to make the journey, and must keep well enough to stay fresh until they arrive at their destination. Don't choose anything fragile (Almond Crescents, for example). Also avoid sticky cookies and those with moist icings or frostings. Crisp cookies are fine if they're not too delicate or crumbly, but the most reliable travelers are firm but not brittle cookies.

The cookies listed below, taken from our selection, are especially good candidates for mailing.

Addendum Cookies (page 21)
English Toffee Squares (page 24)
Twice-baked Walnut Cookies (page 6)
Fruit Bars (page 16)
Poppy Seed Nut Slices (page 25)
Fruitcake Cookie Cups (page 20)
Holiday Date-Nut Drops (page 21)
Nürnberger Lebkuchen (page 17)
Brown Sugar Shortbreads (page 13)
Tutti Frutti Oat Bars (page 22)

Wrapping & mailing

Cookies can be wrapped for travel in several ways. You can wrap them in foil—either individually, in pairs (flat sides together), or in small stacks. Or layer the cookies in containers, such as pretty tins, rigid plastic containers, or attractively wrapped foil loaf or pie pans. Separate layers with wax paper, and pack the cookies securely so they won't jostle about and damage each other in transit. If the container you've chosen isn't airtight, seal it in a plastic bag. Be sure to pack soft and crisp ones separately to preserve their textures.

To pack the cookies for mailing, you'll need a stout box lined with foil or wax paper, and plenty of filler for insulation. For filler, use tightly crumpled newspaper or other paper, or styrofoam packing material. Pad the bottom of the box with several inches of filler; then add foil-wrapped cookies or a cookie-filled tin or container. Make sure to insulate well with filler between packages or around the sides of the container. Add several inches of filler on top of the cookies before closing the box.

The post office requires that all packages be sealed securely with reinforced packing tape; don't use masking tape or transparent tape or tie your package with string. If you like, write "Fragile" and "Perishable" on the box; it may not make any difference in how your cookies are handled, but it can't hurt. Send your package first-class, so your cookies will arrive quickly..

Finnish Ribbon Cakes

(Pictured on page 75)

For holiday entertaining, offer a platter of assorted Scandinavian cookies, such as Spritz (page 8), Finnish Rye Cookies (page 11), Swedish Pinwheel Cookies (page 12), and these fancy morsels.

1 cup (½ lb.) butter or margarine, at room temperature
½ cup granulated sugar
1 large egg yolk
1 teaspoon vanilla
½ teaspoon grated lemon peel
2½ cups all-purpose flour
¼ teaspoon salt

About 6 tablespoons raspberry or apricot jam
½ cup powdered sugar mixed with 1 tablespoon water

In large bowl of an electric mixer, beat butter and granulated sugar until creamy; beat in egg yolk, vanilla, and lemon peel. In another bowl, stir together flour and salt. Gradually add to butter mixture, blending thoroughly.

Shape dough into ropes about ¾ inch in diameter and as long as your baking sheets; place them about 2 inches apart on ungreased baking sheets. With the side of your little finger, press a long groove down center of each rope (don't press all the way down to baking sheets).

Bake cookies in a 375° oven for 10 minutes.

Remove cookies from oven and spoon jam into grooves. Return to oven until cookies are firm to touch and light golden brown (5 to 10 minutes). While cookies are hot, drizzle them with powdered sugar mixture (or spread mixture along sides of cookies). Then cut at a 45° angle into 1-inch lengths. Let cool briefly on baking sheets; transfer to racks and let cool completely. Store airtight. Makes about 4 dozen.

Almond Sculpture Cookies

The cookie collection shown on this page requires a special and versatile dough: one that's malleable in the sculptor's hands, stays tender through shaping and reshaping, holds form and detail in the oven—and finally, when baked, produces a cookie that tastes good.

Substituting almond paste for part of the butter in a shortbread-type dough produces just the right qualities. The almond paste not only adds flavor but also makes the dough pliable, so you can push, poke, and pinch it as you would modeling clay. In addition, it makes the dough firm enough to hold embossed and impressed details.

These cookies are especially fun for children to make. Mistakes in shaping sometimes contribute to a cookie's charm, but if you shape one you don't like, start again; handling won't toughen the dough. Let the illustrated shapes get you started, then go on to create your own figures.

To make shapes like those shown here, you use techniques basic to ceramics—forming slabs, rolling ropes of varying thicknesses, and making impressions with a fork's tines or other objects. To get fine strands, force bits of dough through a well-washed garlic press. For contrasting color, you can use both the golden and cocoa doughs in your creations if you wish.

Let your imagination go *in creating whimsical cookies from an almond-flavored dough that handles like modeling clay; for special effects, combine golden and cocoa doughs. Design: Dora de Larios.*

1 cup (½ lb.) butter or margarine, at room temperature
1 can (8 oz.) almond paste
¾ cup sugar
1 large egg
3 cups all-purpose flour
Cocoa-Almond Sculpture Dough (recipe follows), optional

In large bowl of an electric mixer, beat together butter, almond paste, and sugar until creamy. Beat in egg. Gradually mix in flour until blended. If necessary, cover dough and refrigerate until easy to handle or for up to 3 days.

Form cookies a few at a time, following the general directions above. Shape dough directly on baking sheets, allowing 1 to 2 inches between cookies. For best results, each cookie's maximum thickness should not exceed ¾ inch. Bake in a 300° oven until lightly browned on bottoms (about 20 minutes for ¼-inch-thick cookies, up to 40 minutes for ¾-inch-thick cookies). Let cool briefly on baking sheets, then transfer to racks and let cool completely. Store airtight. Makes about 3⅔ cups dough, enough to make 8 round cookies, each 4 inches in diameter and ½ inch thick.

Cocoa-Almond Sculpture Dough. Follow directions for **Golden Almond Sculpture Cookies**, but decrease flour to 2½ cups and add ½ cup **unsweetened cocoa** with the sugar. Makes about 3¾ cups.

Cutout Cookies

Nothing says "Christmas" like cutout cookies in all the shapes of the season. And few gifts bring more delight than a selection of home-baked, lovingly decorated stars and bells, angels and reindeer—and perhaps a few jaunty gingerbread men with raisin buttons.

We've chosen a variety of rolled and cutout cookies for you here. Some are light and mild-flavored, others dark and spicy; some are crisp, some soft. There are even cookie ornaments with glowing "stained glass" centers—and for the ambitious, a Christmas cabin built of gingerbread logs.

Sugar Cookies

With their pale golden color and delicate vanilla flavor, sugar cookies offer a perfect background for decorating. You can simply sprinkle them with colored sugar, if you like, but it's fun to get a little fancier with icing and other decorations: try a blue-frosted star studded with sparkling silver dragées, or a tree hung with red cinnamon candy "Christmas balls."

Our Easy-to-Cut Cookies let the youngsters join in the fun; they can create their own cookie shapes and choose from a variety of toppings.

> ¾ cup (⅜ lb.) butter or
>   margarine, at room
>   temperature
> 1 cup granulated sugar
> 2 large eggs
> 1 teaspoon vanilla
> 2¾ cups all-purpose flour
> 1 teaspoon **each** baking
>   powder and salt
>   Red or green decorating
>   sugar; or granulated
>   sugar

In large bowl of an electric mixer, beat butter and the 1 cup granulated sugar until creamy; beat in eggs and vanilla. In another bowl, stir together flour, baking powder, and salt; gradually add to butter mixture, blending thoroughly, to form a soft dough. Cover tightly with plastic wrap and refrigerate until firm (at least 1 hour) or for up to 3 days.

On a floured board, roll out dough, a portion at a time, to a thickness of ⅛ inch (keep remaining portions refrigerated). Cut out with cookie cutters (about 2½ inches in diameter) and place slightly apart on ungreased baking sheets. Sprinkle with red or green sugar.

Bake in a 400° oven until edges are lightly browned (8 to 10 minutes). Transfer to racks and let cool completely before handling. Store airtight. Makes about 4 dozen.

Easy-to-Cut Cookies

Let children choose one or more fairly simple cookie shapes—block letters, numbers, or shapes such as triangles, squares, and circles. Then trace or draw shapes on sturdy cardboard (about ⅟₁₆ inch thick), making each one about 3 by 5 inches. Cut out patterns with scissors, making sure edges are smooth.

Prepare dough as directed for **Sugar Cookies**; divide into 12 equal portions. On a floured board or directly on a lightly floured baking sheet, roll out each portion to a thickness of ⅛ inch. Let children cut around patterns with a dull knife; then lift off excess dough and set aside to reroll for additional cookies. Offer toppings such as **raisins**, **chocolate chips**, whole or chopped **nuts**, **sunflower seeds**, and **flaked coconut** for embellishing cookies. Bake as directed for **Sugar Cookies**. Makes about 2 dozen.

Finnish Rye Cookies

Rye flour gives these cookies their unusual nutty flavor. The shape is a bit unusual, too—each thin round has a small, off-center hole cut in it. In Finland, where they're a Christmas tradition, the cookies are known as *ruiskakut*.

> 1 cup rye flour
> ½ cup all-purpose flour
> ¼ teaspoon salt
> ½ cup sugar
> ½ cup (¼ lb.) firm butter
>   or margarine, cut into
>   pieces
> ¼ cup milk

In a bowl, stir together rye flour, all-purpose flour, salt, and sugar. Add butter and rub in with your fingers until mixture forms fine, even crumbs. Add milk, 1 tablespoon at a time, stirring with a fork until a stiff dough forms. Gather dough into a ball, wrap tightly in plastic wrap, and refrigerate for 1 hour.

On a floured board, roll out dough, a portion at a time, to a thickness of about ⅛ inch. Cut out with a round cookie cutter (about 2½ inches in diameter). Then cut a hole slightly off center in each cookie, using a tiny round cutter about ½ inch in diameter (you can use the cap from a vanilla or other extract bottle). Place slightly apart on lightly greased baking sheets; prick each cookie several times with a fork. (You can bake the little cut-out holes, too—or reroll them to make more cookies.)

Bake in a 375° oven until cookies are lightly browned and firm to the touch (8 to 10 minutes). Transfer baked cookies to racks and let cool. Store airtight. Makes about 2½ dozen.

Swedish Pinwheel Cookies

Rich cookies like these fancy but easily formed pinwheels are favorites in Sweden at Christmas. They have a tender, flaky texture that's achieved by cutting butter into flour as you would for pastry, then rolling and folding the dough several times to make buttery layers.

1   cup (½ lb.) firm butter
     or margarine, cut into
     small pieces
2   cups all-purpose flour
3   tablespoons cold water
     About ½ cup thick
     preserves or jam
1   large egg, beaten
     About ½ cup crushed
     sugar cubes

With a pastry blender or 2 knives, cut butter into flour until fat particles are about the size of peas. Sprinkle in water, stirring with a fork until dough pulls away from bowl; gather into a ball. Wrap tightly in plastic wrap and refrigerate for at least 1 hour.

On a lightly floured board, roll dough into a 14-inch square. Fold square in half and roll into a 7- by 21-inch rectangle; fold in thirds, overlapping layers to make a 7-inch square. Repeat this rolling and folding procedure 2 more times, ending with a 7-inch square. Wrap and refrigerate for at least 30 minutes.

Roll dough into a 14-inch square on a lightly floured board. Using a pastry wheel, trim off any uneven edges; then cut large square into 25 small squares, each about 2¾ inches on a side. Cut in diagonally from all 4 corners of each square almost to center. Place 1 teaspoon preserves in center of each square. At center, overlap alternate corners to form pinwheels; pinch together firmly.

Brush pinwheels all over with egg, then sprinkle with sugar. Place several inches apart on greased baking sheets and bake in a 400° oven until lightly browned (about 12 minutes). Let cookies cool on baking sheets for 3 minutes; transfer to racks and let cool completely. Store airtight. Makes 25.

Cookie Canvases

These sturdy cookies make perfect canvases for food-coloring artists of all ages. They're a diverting, delicious project for a casual Christmas party—and when it's time to go home, guests can take their "edible masterpieces" with them.

You'll need to bake the cookies ahead of time, since they're coated with a glaze that must dry for 8 to 24 hours. When it's time to paint, provide several sizes of watercolor brushes, clear water for rinsing them, and small cups of food color—undiluted for bright colors, slightly diluted with water for lighter colors. To prevent colors from bleeding together, let each color dry briefly before painting another over it.

2   cups (1 lb.) butter or
     margarine, at room
     temperature
2   cups granulated sugar
2   teaspoons vanilla
5   cups all-purpose flour
1   to 1½ pounds powdered
     sugar
6   to 9 tablespoons warm
     water
     Assorted food colors

In large bowl of an electric mixer, beat butter, granulated sugar, and vanilla until creamy. Beat in flour until thoroughly combined. With a floured, stockinet-covered rolling pin, roll out enough dough on an ungreased unrimmed baking sheet to cover sheet in a ¼- to ⅜-inch-thick layer.

For rectangular or square cookies, use a sharp knife and a ruler to cut away a 1-inch strip of dough on all sides of baking sheet; make no other cuts. For round or decorative shapes, use large floured cookie cutters (or use a coffee or tuna can with both ends removed). Cut shapes, leaving at least 1 inch between cookies and lifting away excess dough.

Combine trimmings with remaining dough; then repeat rolling and cutting until all dough is used. Bake in a 300° oven until cookies are pale gold and centers are firm to the touch (25 to 30 minutes).

Meanwhile, place powdered sugar in a large bowl. Gradually add water (about 6 tablespoons per pound), beating constantly, until glaze is smooth and thick; mixture should flow smoothly but set quickly.

Remove cookies from oven. If making rectangles or squares, cut while still hot, using a sharp knife and a ruler; trim to straighten edges. Let cookies of all shapes cool on baking sheets until just warm to the touch (about 7 minutes).

With a wide spatula, transfer cookies to a flat foil-covered surface. Quickly spread each cookie with enough glaze to make a very smooth surface. Do not cover or move cookies until glaze is dry to the touch (8 to 24 hours).

Paint with food colors. Or stack unpainted cookies between pieces of foil and wrap airtight; store at room temperature for up to 4 days, or freeze for longer storage. (If frozen, unwrap and let thaw at room temperature before painting.) Makes about 1 dozen 6-inch cookies or 2 dozen 3- to 4-inch cookies.

Gingerbread Boys

(Pictured on page 15)

Before baking these spicy gingerbread boys, you move the arms and legs to give the figures a lively air and a lot of personality. If you like, punch a hole for hanging in each one; the baked cookies make charming ornaments for your Christmas tree.

- ½ cup (¼ lb.) butter or margarine, at room temperature
- 1 cup firmly packed brown sugar
- 1½ cups light molasses
- ⅔ cup water or apple juice
- 6½ cups all-purpose flour
- 2 teaspoons *each* baking soda and salt
- 1 teaspoon *each* ground cinnamon, ginger, cloves, and allspice
  Raisins
- 1 large egg white, lightly beaten
  Purchased decorating icing in a tube or aerosol can

In large bowl of an electric mixer, beat butter and sugar until creamy. Add molasses and beat until blended, then mix in water. In another bowl, stir together flour, baking soda, salt, cinnamon, ginger, cloves, and all spice. Gradually add to butter mixture, blending to form a stiff dough. Cover tightly with plastic wrap and refrigerate for several hours or until next day.

On a floured board, roll out dough, a portion at a time, to a thickness of ³⁄₁₆ inch. Cut out with a 4- to 6-inch gingerbread boy cutter and, with cutter still in place, transfer cookie and cutter with a wide spatula to a lightly greased baking sheet. Lift off cutter and repeat. If desired, insert a short length of plastic drinking straw into each cookie near the top to make a hole for hanging; press straw all the way through to baking sheet. Leave straws in place while baking.

Dip raisins in egg white and press them firmly into dough to make buttons (use about 3 per cookie). Move arms and legs to animate the figures.

Bake in a 350° oven until lightly browned (10 to 15 minutes). Transfer cookies to racks, remove straws (if used), and let cool completely. Draw faces on cooled cookies with icing. Tie ribbon or thread through holes for hanging, if desired. Store airtight. Makes about 4 dozen.

Sour Cream Spice Cookies

Ground coriander lends a warm, sweet spiciness to these tender sour cream cookies. For variety, you can top the cutouts with pine nuts and a sprinkling of sugar.

- ½ cup (¼ lb.) butter or margarine, at room temperature
- 1 cup sugar
- 1 large egg
- ½ teaspoon *each* vanilla and almond extract
- ½ teaspoon baking soda
- ½ cup sour cream
- 3 cups all-purpose flour
- 1½ teaspoons baking powder
- ½ teaspoon *each* salt and ground coriander

In large bowl of an electric mixer, beat butter and sugar until creamy; beat in egg, vanilla, and almond extract. Stir baking soda into sour cream, then beat into butter mixture. In another bowl, stir together flour, baking powder, salt, and coriander; gradually add to butter mixture, blending thoroughly. Cover tightly with plastic wrap and refrigerate until firm (about 1 hour) or for up to 3 days.

On a lightly floured board, roll out half the dough to a thickness of about ⅛ inch. Cut out with cookie cutters (about 2½ inches in diameter) and place slightly apart on ungreased baking sheets. Repeat with remaining dough. Bake in a 400° oven until golden (8 to 10 minutes). Transfer to racks and let cool. Store airtight. Makes about 5 dozen.

Pine Nut Sugar Cookies

Prepare dough and cut out cookies as directed for **Sour Cream Spice Cookies**, but place on greased baking sheets. Beat 1 large **egg** with 1 teaspoon **water** and brush over cookies; then press **pine nuts** into surface of cookies (you'll need about ½ cup). Sprinkle cookies lightly with **sugar** and bake in a 375° oven until edges are golden (about 10 minutes).

Brown Sugar Shortbreads

You need just four ingredients to make these buttery brown sugar cookies. To give them a festive air, you might top each with a dot of buttercream frosting and half a candied cherry.

- 1 cup (½ lb.) butter or margarine, at room temperature
- 1¼ cups firmly packed brown sugar
- 1 teaspoon vanilla
- 2½ cups all-purpose flour

In large bowl of an electric mixer, beat butter and sugar until creamy. Add vanilla; then gradually beat in flour, blending thoroughly. Gather dough into a ball, wrap tightly in plastic wrap, and refrigerate until firm (about 1 hour) or for up to 3 days.

On a lightly floured board, roll out dough to a thickness of ¼ inch. Cut out with cookie cutters (about 2½ inches in diameter) and place slightly apart on lightly greased baking sheets. Bake in a 300° oven until firm to the touch (35 to 40 minutes; press very lightly to test). Transfer to racks and let cool. Store airtight. Makes about 3 dozen.

Stained-glass Cookies
(Pictured on facing page)

Shimmering red or green candy centers accent these crisp cutout cookies. Each one has a loop of ribbon attached so you can hang them on your Christmas tree or tie them to gifts as edible decorations. The cookies are made from a sour cream dough flavored with nutmeg—but if you prefer, you can substitute the dough used for our Gingerbread Log Cabin (page 18).

For shaping, you'll need a 4-inch round cookie cutter (or a tuna can with ends removed) and some smaller cutters for making the center cutouts. Also have ready about 7½ yards of ¼-inch ribbon for hanging.

Though these ornaments are quite durable, their candy centers may run if you hang them near a hot light or where humidity is high. To prevent this, we recommend heat-sealing the cookies in plastic wrap (directions follow).

½ cup (¼ lb.) butter or
    margarine, at room
    temperature
½ *cup solid vegetable*
    shortening
1½ *cups sugar*
½ *cup sour cream*
1 *teaspoon vanilla*
1 *large egg*
3¾ *cups all-purpose flour*
1 *teaspoon ground*
    nutmeg
½ *teaspoon **each** baking*
    soda and salt
2 *cups sugar*
1 *cup light corn syrup*
½ *cup water*
    Red or green food color
½ *to 1 teaspoon flavoring,*
    such as raspberry,
    peppermint, or pineapple

In large bowl of an electric mixer, beat butter, shortening, and the 1½ cups sugar until creamy; beat in sour cream, vanilla, and egg. In another bowl, stir together flour, nutmeg, baking soda, and salt; gradually add to butter mixture, blending thoroughly. Cover dough tightly with plastic wrap and refrigerate until next day.

Divide dough into quarters. Work with 1 portion at a time; keep remaining dough refrigerated until ready to roll. Roll out on a floured board to a thickness of ⅛ inch. Cut out with a 4-inch round cookie cutter and transfer to greased baking sheets, spacing cookies about 1 inch apart. Refrigerate sheets. When cookies are cold, cut out centers with a smaller cutter. Refrigerate scraps to reroll with remaining dough.

Bake cookies in a 375° oven just until firm but not yet browned around edges (6 to 7 minutes). Let cool on baking sheets for 5 minutes; transfer to a flat surface and let cool completely.

Cut ¼-inch ribbon into 8-inch lengths. Loop a piece of ribbon through center of each cooled cookie; tie securely at top. Arrange cookies, right side up, on greased baking sheets.

For candy centers, place two 1-cup glass measuring cups in a 375° oven to preheat. Combine the 2 cups sugar, corn syrup, and water in a 2-quart pan. Cook over medium-high heat, stirring, until sugar is dissolved. Then cook without stirring until syrup reaches 280°F (hard crack stage) on a candy thermometer. Remove from heat; stir in your choice of food color and flavoring.

Remove 1 measuring cup from oven; fill with half the syrup (keep remaining syrup over low heat). As soon as syrup in cup stops bubbling, hold cup with a potholder and pour syrup in a thin stream to fill cookie centers. Repeat, using second cup and remaining syrup. Let cookies cool completely; twist gently to loosen, then slide off sheets. Store airtight in a single layer in a cool, dry place, or heat-seal in plastic wrap (see below). Makes about 2½ dozen.

To heat-seal, lay a piece of brown paper (or a piece of paper bag) on a baking sheet. Set sheet in oven and heat to 300°. Tear plastic wrap into 8-inch lengths. Wrap each cookie; secure with cellophane tape. Place about 4 cookies at a time, right sides up, on paper; close oven door for 20 seconds. Remove and let cool.

Nutmeg Crisps

Made from a buttermilk dough and flavored with ground nutmeg, these simple cookies go well with tea, coffee, or holiday eggnog. For extra-fresh nutmeg flavor, try buying whole nutmeg and grating it yourself.

1 *cup (½ lb.) butter or*
    margarine, at room
    temperature
1 *cup sugar*
1 *large egg*
3½ *cups all-purpose flour*
⅛ *teaspoon salt*
1 *teaspoon **each** ground*
    nutmeg and baking
    soda
½ *cup buttermilk*

In large bowl of an electric mixer, beat butter and sugar until creamy; beat in egg until well combined. In another bowl, stir together flour, salt, nutmeg, and baking soda; add to butter mixture alternately with buttermilk, beating thoroughly after each addition. Gather dough into a ball, wrap tightly in plastic wrap, and refrigerate until firm (2 to 3 hours) or for up to 3 days.

On a well-floured board, roll out dough, a portion at a time, to a thickness of about ⅛ inch (keep remaining portions refrigerated). Cut out with cookie cutters (about 2½ inches in diameter) and place slightly apart on ungreased baking sheets.

Bake in a 350° oven until lightly browned (about 10 minutes). Transfer to racks and let cool. Store airtight. Makes about 7 dozen.

Dear Santa Claus
I would like a
dollhouse and a Kitten
and a pony for
hristmas.
Thank you.
Love, Alexandra

Santa is sure to feel welcome *when he sees the tree decorated with Anise Pretzels (page 5), Gingerbread Boys (page 13), and Stained-glass Cookies (facing page). Nürnberger Lebkuchen (page 17) and Fruitcake Cookie Cups (page 20) make tempting accompaniments for steaming hot cocoa.*

Fruit Bars

When you're choosing cookies to mail to faraway friends, don't forget these tender, fruit-filled bars. They become softer and more flavorful a day or two after baking—so they'll arrive at their destination tasting perfectly delicious.

- ½ cup (¼ lb.) butter or margarine, at room temperature
- ½ cup **each** granulated sugar and firmly packed brown sugar
- 2 large eggs
- ½ teaspoon vanilla
- 1 cup whole wheat flour
- 1¼ cups all-purpose flour
- ¼ cup toasted unsweetened wheat germ
- ¼ teaspoon **each** salt and baking soda
  Fruit Filling (recipes follow)

In large bowl of an electric mixer, beat butter, granulated sugar, and brown sugar until creamy. Beat in eggs and vanilla. In another bowl, stir together whole wheat flour, all-purpose flour, wheat germ, salt, and baking soda; gradually add to butter mixture, blending thoroughly.

Cover dough tightly with plastic wrap and refrigerate until easy to handle (at least 1 hour) or until next day.

Divide dough into 2 equal portions. Return 1 portion to refrigerator. On a floured board, roll out other portion to a straight-edged 9- by 15-inch rectangle; cut lengthwise into 3 strips.

Divide cooled Fruit Filling of your choice into 6 equal portions and evenly distribute 1 portion down center of each strip, bringing it out to ends. Use a long spatula to lift sides of each dough strip over filling, overlapping edges slightly on top. Press together lightly. Cut strips in half crosswise; lift and invert onto greased baking sheets (seam side should be down). Brush off excess flour. Refrigerate for about 15 minutes. Meanwhile, repeat rolling and filling with remaining dough.

Bake in a 375° oven until browned (15 to 20 minutes). Let cool on baking sheets on a rack for about 10 minutes; then cut each strip crosswise into 4 pieces. Transfer cookies to racks and let cool completely. Store covered. Makes 4 dozen.

Fig Filling. Using a food processor or a food chopper fitted with a medium blade, grind together 1 pound **dried figs** (about 2 cups lightly packed) and ½ cup **walnuts** or almonds. Turn into a medium-size pan and add ⅓ cup **sugar**, ½ cup **water**, 1 teaspoon grated **lemon peel**, and 2 tablespoons **lemon juice**. Place over medium heat and cook, stirring, until mixture boils and becomes very thick (5 to 8 minutes). Let cool completely.

Prune Filling. Follow directions for **Fig Filling**, but substitute 2 cups lightly packed **moist-pack pitted prunes** for figs and add ¾ teaspoon **ground cinnamon** with sugar.

Apricot Filling. Follow directions for **Fig Filling**, but substitute 3 cups lightly packed **dried apricots** for figs and use 1 teaspoon grated **orange peel** in place of lemon peel.

Date Filling. Follow directions for **Fig Filling**, but substitute 1 pound **pitted dates** for figs and increase lemon peel to 2 teaspoons.

Anise Cookies

If you enjoy the flavor of anise, you'll want to add these crisp cutouts to your holiday baking. They're made with anise sugar: plain granulated sugar that has been mixed with anise seeds, then allowed to stand for a day. When you make the cookies, you can add the seeds to the dough along with the sugar, or sift them out first for a subtler flavor.

- ¾ cup sugar
- 2 teaspoons anise seeds
- 1 cup (½ lb.) butter or margarine, at room temperature
- 1 large egg
- 2 tablespoons brandy or 1 tablespoon **each** lemon juice and water
- 3 cups all-purpose flour
- 1 teaspoon baking powder
- ½ teaspoon **each** salt and ground cinnamon

Combine sugar and anise seeds; cover tightly and let stand for about 24 hours. Sift out and discard seeds, if desired.

In large bowl of an electric mixer, beat butter and ½ cup of the anise sugar until creamy. Beat in egg and brandy. In another bowl, stir together flour, baking powder, salt, and cinnamon; gradually add to butter mixture, blending thoroughly. Gather dough into a ball, wrap tightly in plastic wrap, and refrigerate until firm (about 1 hour) or for up to 3 days.

Roll out dough on a lightly floured board to a thickness of ⅛ inch. Cut out with cookie cutters (about 2½ inches in diameter) and place 1 inch apart on lightly greased baking sheets. Sift and discard seeds from remaining ¼ cup anise sugar (if you haven't already done so) and sprinkle sugar evenly over cookies.

Bake in a 350° oven until golden brown (about 12 minutes). Transfer to racks and let cool. Store airtight. Makes about 5 dozen.

Almond Ravioli Cookies

(Pictured on page 7)

Do you need a big batch of cookies for a big party? Try these little almond-filled bites. To make them, you use a ravioli-making technique familiar from Italian cooking: roll out one sheet of dough, top with dots of filling, and press on a second sheet of dough. Then just cut the cookies—about 150 of them!—apart.

1   cup (½ lb.) butter or margarine, at room temperature
1½ cups powdered sugar
1   large egg
1   teaspoon vanilla
2½ cups all-purpose flour
1   teaspoon **each** baking soda and cream of tartar
    About ⅔ cup almond paste
    About ⅓ cup sliced almonds

In large bowl of an electric mixer, beat butter and sugar until creamy; beat in egg and vanilla. In another bowl, stir together flour, baking soda, and cream of tartar; gradually add to butter mixture, blending thoroughly. Divide dough in half. Wrap each half tightly in plastic wrap and refrigerate until firm (2 to 3 hours) or for up to 3 days.

Place 1 portion of dough between 2 pieces of wax paper and roll out to a 10- by 15-inch rectangle. Peel off and discard top paper.

With a pastry wheel or a long-bladed knife, lightly mark dough into 1-inch squares. Place a small ball of almond paste (use a scant ¼ teaspoon for each) in the center of each square; refrigerate while rolling top layer.

Repeat rolling procedure for second portion of dough. Peel off and discard top paper. Invert sheet of dough onto almond-paste-topped dough. Peel off and discard paper.

Gently press top layer of dough around mounds of filling.

Flour a pastry wheel or sharp knife and cut filled dough into 1-inch squares, then run pastry wheel around outer edges to seal (or press with fingers). Place cookies about 1 inch apart on ungreased baking sheets. Push a sliced almond diagonally into center of each cookie.

Bake in a 350° oven until golden (10 to 12 minutes). Transfer to racks and let cool. Store airtight. Makes about 12½ dozen.

Nürnberger Lebkuchen

(Pictured on page 15)

In Nürnberg, Germany, Christmas baking begins in November with the preparation of *lebkuchen*—spicy, cakelike honey cookies that need to age for several weeks to become soft and chewy.

1   cup honey
¾   cup firmly packed dark brown sugar
1   large egg, lightly beaten
1   tablespoon lemon juice
1   teaspoon grated lemon peel
2⅓ cups all-purpose flour
1   teaspoon ground cinnamon
½   teaspoon **each** ground allspice, cloves, and nutmeg
½   teaspoon **each** salt and baking soda
⅓   cup **each** finely chopped candied citron and finely chopped almonds
    About 24 candied cherries, cut in half
6   to 8 ounces whole blanched almonds
    Rum Glaze (recipe follows)

Heat honey in a small pan over medium-high heat just until it begins to bubble. Remove from heat and let cool slightly. Stir in sugar, egg, lemon juice, and lemon peel; let cool to lukewarm.

In a large bowl, stir together flour, cinnamon, allspice, cloves, nutmeg, salt, and baking soda. Add honey mixture, citron, and chopped almonds; stir until well blended (dough will be soft). Cover tightly with plastic wrap and refrigerate for at least 8 hours or for up to 2 days.

Work with ¼ of the dough at a time, keeping remaining dough refrigerated. On a heavily floured board, roll out dough with a floured rolling pin to a thickness of ⅜ inch. Cut dough with a 2½-inch round cookie cutter; place cookies 2 inches apart on baking sheets lined with lightly greased parchment paper.

Press a cherry half into center of each cookie; surround with 3 almonds arranged like flower petals. Bake in a 375° oven until golden brown (12 to 15 minutes). Remove cookies from oven and immediately brush Rum Glaze over tops with a pastry brush; transfer to racks and let cool. As soon as top glaze dries, turn cookies over and brush glaze over bottoms.

When cookies are completely cooled and dry, pack into airtight containers and store at room temperature for at least 2 weeks or for up to 3 months. If cookies get slightly hard, add a thin slice of apple to each container; cover tightly and store until cookies are moist again (about 1 day), then discard apple. Makes about 4 dozen.

Rum Glaze. Stir together 1 cup **powdered sugar** and 5 tablespoons **rum** or water until very smooth.

Gingerbread Log Cabin
(Pictured below)

Surrounded with soft powdered-sugar snowdrifts, this little cabin makes an enchanting centerpiece for a children's Christmas party. It's easily assembled from gingerbread "logs" cut out with homemade cardboard patterns; you'll also need a 12-inch square of stiff cardboard for a foundation. Complete the edible winter wonderland with decorative details cut from leftover dough. Or use your favorite holiday decorations—tiny Christmas trees, figurines, toy reindeer, and the like.

- ¾ cup solid vegetable shortening
- ¾ cup granulated sugar
- ¾ cup molasses
- 2 tablespoons water
- 3¼ cups all-purpose flour
- 1 teaspoon **each** salt, baking soda, and ground ginger
- ¼ teaspoon **each** ground nutmeg and allspice
  White Icing (recipe follows)
  About 4 cups powdered sugar

In large bowl of an electric mixer, beat shortening and granulated sugar until creamy; beat in molasses and water. In another bowl, stir together

Set in a drift of powdered-sugar "snow," our charming Gingerbread Log Cabin is certain to delight grownups and children alike.

flour, salt, baking soda, ginger, nutmeg, and allspice; gradually add to shortening mixture, blending thoroughly. Cover tightly with plastic wrap and refrigerate until firm (about 2 hours).

Meanwhile, prepare foundation for cabin by covering a 12-inch square of stiff cardboard with foil. Also prepare patterns for cutting logs: cut lightweight cardboard into a 4- by 6-inch rectangle (for the roof); ½-inch-wide strips that are 2, 3½, and 6 inches long (for logs); and a ½-inch square (for spacers).

With a floured rolling pin, roll out ⅓ of the dough on a floured board to a thickness of ⅛ inch (keep remaining dough refrigerated). Make 2 roof sections by cutting around roof pattern with a sharp knife; transfer carefully to a lightly greased baking sheet.

Roll out scraps and all remaining dough to a thickness of ⅜ inch. Then cut out eight 2-inch-long logs, two 3½-inch-long logs, seventeen 6-inch-long logs, and 30 spacers (½-inch squares). Transfer cookies to lightly greased baking sheets (bake separately from roof sections), arranging about 1 inch apart. From remaining dough, cut out trees or other decorative details. Extra spacers can be used for chimney and stepping stones.

Bake in a 350° oven until just firm to the touch (12 to 15 minutes; cookies will harden as they cool). As soon as roof section is baked, lay pattern on each section and evenly trim 1 long edge (where the 2 sections will meet). Let cookies cool briefly on baking sheets, then transfer to racks and let cool completely. If not assembling cabin at once, package airtight; freeze if desired.

With a pastry brush, paint foil-covered foundation with White Icing, then sift some of the powdered sugar over icing to cover lightly.

To assemble cabin, start with a 6-inch log in back, two 2-inch logs in front. Top with 6-inch logs on sides, letting ends extend; use icing as glue where logs join. Continue building in this way for 2 more layers, using spacers at inner edges of 2-inch logs and gluing with icing as needed.

For the fourth layer, use 6-inch logs all around. Add 3 spacers across the doorway; then top with 6-inch logs across front and back.

Using spacers and 3½- and 2½-inch logs, build up gables on front and back of cabin. Place a spacer atop each gable.

Ice roof pieces and sift sugar over them. Ice top logs and spacers; set roof in place, trimmed edges together.

Decorate cabin and its grounds as desired with extra shapes. In most dry climates, cabin will keep for about 1 week. In humid areas, cookies may absorb moisture and start to sag, so plan to keep cabin for only 2 or 3 days before eating.

White Icing. In a bowl, beat together 2 cups **powdered sugar** and ¼ cup **water** until smooth.

Swedish Ginger Thins
(Pictured on page 75)

Very spicy, very dark, very thin, and very crisp—these are the words to describe *pepparkakor,* Sweden's version of gingersnaps. For the holidays, cut them into fancy shapes; then dress them up further with decorative icing, if you like.

- ⅔ cup (⅓ lb.) butter or margarine
- ⅓ cup **each** granulated sugar and firmly packed brown sugar
- 2 tablespoons dark corn syrup
- 2 teaspoons **each** ground ginger and cloves
- 1 tablespoon ground cinnamon
- 2 teaspoons baking soda
- ¼ cup water
- 2½ cups all-purpose flour
  Royal Icing (recipe follows) or purchased decorating icing in a tube or aerosol can (optional)
  Multicolored candy sprinkles (optional)

In a medium-size pan, combine butter, granulated sugar, brown sugar, and corn syrup; place over medium heat and stir until butter is melted. Remove from heat, stir in ginger, cloves, and cinnamon, and let cool slightly. Stir baking soda into water and add to butter mixture, blending thoroughly. Then stir in flour until well combined (dough will be quite soft). Cover tightly with plastic wrap and refrigerate until firm (2 to 3 hours) or for up to 3 days.

On a floured board, roll out dough, a portion at a time, to a thickness of about ¹⁄₁₆ inch. Cut out with cookie cutters (about 2½ inches in diameter). If necessary, dip cutters in flour to prevent dough from sticking to them. Place cookies slightly apart on ungreased baking sheets. Bake in a 325° oven until slightly darker brown and firm to the touch (10 to 12 minutes). Transfer to racks and let cool completely.

If desired, press Royal Icing through a decorating tube, making swirls or other designs on cookies. Decorate icing with candy sprinkles, if desired. Let icing dry before storing cookies. Store airtight. Makes about 5 dozen.

Royal Icing. In small bowl of an electric mixer, beat 1 large **egg white** with ⅛ teaspoon **cream of tartar** and a dash of **salt** for 1 minute on high speed. Add 2 cups **powdered sugar** and beat slowly until blended; then beat on high speed until very stiff (3 to 5 minutes).

Drop Cookies

If your children like to help with the holiday baking, be sure to mix up a batch or two of drop cookies. Shaping couldn't be easier; you just drop the dough from a spoon onto baking sheets or, in the case of our Fruitcake Cookie Cups, into small paper bonbon cups. Most of the choices here are chunky with fruit, nuts, and other goodies, but you'll find some plainer cookies, too—like golden Bourbon Chews.

Bourbon Chews

These cookies are spirited in more ways than one. Molasses and ginger provide part of their spicy character; bourbon whiskey does the rest.

- 1 cup all-purpose flour
- ½ cup sugar
- 1 teaspoon ground ginger
- ¼ teaspoon salt
- ⅓ cup light molasses
- ½ cup (¼ lb.) butter or margarine
- 3 tablespoons bourbon whiskey
- ¼ cup chopped almonds or walnuts

In a small bowl, stir together flour, sugar, ginger, and salt; set aside. In a 1-quart pan, bring molasses to a boil over high heat; add butter and stir until melted. Remove from heat and stir in flour mixture, bourbon, and almonds until batter is smooth and well combined.

Drop batter by level tablespoonfuls onto greased baking sheets, spacing cookies about 3 inches apart; then spread each into a 2-inch circle with the back of a spoon. Bake in a 300° oven until cookies look dry and are no longer sticky to the touch (8 to 10 minutes). Let cool on baking sheets for about 3 minutes, then transfer to racks and let cool completely. Store airtight. Makes about 2 dozen.

Fruitcake Cookie Cups
(Pictured on page 15)

Like miniature Christmas fruitcakes, these moist cookies age well. You bake them in little paper bonbon cups, available in cookware shops.

- ¼ cup (⅛ lb.) butter or margarine, at room temperature
- ½ cup firmly packed brown sugar
- ¼ cup apple jelly or red currant jelly
- 2 large eggs
- 1 teaspoon vanilla
- 1½ cups all-purpose flour
- 2 teaspoons baking soda
- ½ teaspoon **each** ground allspice, cloves, cinnamon, and nutmeg
- 1 cup chopped walnuts or pecans
- 1 cup currants or raisins
- 1 cup chopped candied cherries or mixed candied fruit

In large bowl of an electric mixer, beat butter and sugar until creamy; beat in jelly, eggs, and vanilla. In another bowl, stir together flour, baking soda, allspice, cloves, cinnamon, and nutmeg. Blend half the flour mixture into butter mixture. Add walnuts, currants, and cherries to remaining flour mixture; then stir into butter mixture, blending thoroughly.

Spoon 1½ to 2 teaspoons batter into each paper bonbon cup and place about 1 inch apart on baking sheets; or drop batter by rounded teaspoonfuls directly onto lightly greased baking sheets, spacing cookies about 2 inches apart. Bake in a 300° oven until centers spring back when lightly touched (17 to 20 minutes). Let cool on racks. Store airtight. Makes about 6 dozen.

Glazed Mincemeat Drops

Old-fashioned mincemeat recipes usually call for beef and suet. These cookies are made with purchased mincemeat, which contains mainly fruit and sweeteners with little or no meat—but they still boast traditional spicy flavor and festive seasonal appeal.

- 1 cup (½ lb.) butter or margarine, at room temperature
- 1½ cups firmly packed brown sugar
- 3 large eggs
- 3 cups all-purpose flour
- ½ teaspoon **each** baking powder and salt
- 1 teaspoon **each** baking soda and ground cinnamon
- 1 cup rolled oats
- 2 cups prepared mincemeat
- 1 cup chopped walnuts
  Spicy Glaze
  (recipe follows)

In large bowl of an electric mixer, beat butter and sugar until creamy; beat in eggs. In another bowl, stir together flour, baking powder, salt, baking soda, cinnamon, and oats. Gradually add to butter mixture, blending thoroughly. Stir in mincemeat and walnuts.

Drop dough by level tablespoonfuls onto greased baking sheets, spacing cookies 3 inches apart. Bake in a 400° oven until golden brown (8 to 10 minutes).

Transfer cookies to racks. Prepare Spicy Glaze and spread over tops of cookies while they're still warm; let cool completely. Store airtight. Makes 6 to 7 dozen.

Spicy Glaze. In a bowl, stir together 3 cups **powdered sugar**, ¾ teaspoon **ground cinnamon**, and 3 tablespoons *each* **brandy** and **water** (or 6 tablespoons water) until smooth.

Addendum Cookies

Holiday time calls for cookies—often lots of different cookies, in not much time. If you need to turn out a variety of cookies quickly, you've found the right recipe. You make one basic dough and divide it up, then stir your choice of additions into each portion of dough—and presto, several different kinds of cookies from one batch!

1 cup (½ lb.) butter or margarine, at room temperature
1 cup *each* granulated sugar and firmly packed brown sugar
2 large eggs
2 teaspoons vanilla
2½ cups all-purpose flour
1 teaspoon baking soda
½ teaspoon salt
    Addenda (suggestions follow)

In large bowl of an electric mixer, beat butter, granulated sugar, and brown sugar until creamy; then beat in eggs and vanilla. In another bowl, stir together flour, baking soda, and salt; gradually add to butter mixture, blending thoroughly. Divide dough in half and mix 1 addendum into each portion. (You may also divide dough into quarters, then mix half an addendum into each quarter; or double an addendum and mix it into the entire batch of dough.)

Drop dough by rounded teaspoonfuls onto ungreased baking sheets, spacing cookies 2 inches apart. Bake in a 350° oven until just set in center when lightly touched (12 to 15 minutes). Transfer to racks and let cool. Store airtight. Makes 8 to 10 dozen.

Addenda. Stir one of the following into each half of the dough:

- 2 ounces **unsweetened chocolate**, melted and cooled, and ½ cup finely crushed **hard peppermint candy**.
- 2 ounces **unsweetened chocolate**, melted and cooled, 1½ teaspoons **rum flavoring**, and ½ cup crushed **peanut brittle** or chopped salted peanuts.
- ¼ cup **sour cream**, 1 teaspoon **ground nutmeg**, and ½ cup dry-roasted **sunflower seeds**.
- 1 cup **rolled oats**, 1 teaspoon grated **orange peel**, ¼ cup **orange juice**, and ½ cup **raisins** or snipped pitted dates.
- ½ cup **applesauce**, ½ cup **wheat germ** or crushed ready-to-eat cereal flakes, ½ cup chopped **nuts**, and 1 teaspoon **pumpkin pie spice** or ground cinnamon.
- 1 cup **granola-style cereal** (break up any large lumps before measuring), 1 cup snipped **pitted dates** or dried apricots, 1 teaspoon **ground cinnamon**, and ¼ cup **milk**.

Holiday Date-Nut Drops

Much like Fruitcake Cookie Cups (see facing page), these tender drops are studded with nuts and fruit. For a party-pretty finish, top each cookie with a walnut half or candied cherry before baking.

½ cup (¼ lb.) butter or margarine, at room temperature
1 cup firmly packed brown sugar
1 large egg
1 teaspoon vanilla
1⅔ cups all-purpose flour
½ teaspoon baking soda
¼ teaspoon salt
¼ cup buttermilk
½ cup chopped walnuts
1 cup quartered red or green candied cherries (or some of each)
1 cup snipped pitted dates
1 cup raisins
    Walnut halves or red or green candied cherry halves

In large bowl of an electric mixer, beat butter and sugar until fluffy. Beat in egg and vanilla. In another bowl, stir together flour, baking soda, and salt; add to creamed mixture alternately with buttermilk. Stir in chopped walnuts, quartered cherries, dates, and raisins.

Drop dough by generous teaspoonfuls onto greased baking sheets, spacing cookies about 2 inches apart. Top each cookie with a walnut or cherry half. Bake in a 375° oven until centers spring back when lightly pressed (8 to 10 minutes). Transfer to racks and let cool. Store airtight. Makes about 5 dozen.

Bar Cookies

Baked in a pan, then cut into strips, squares, or triangles, bar cookies are both simple to make and ideal for carrying to parties. Here's a handful of choices, from crisp English Toffee Squares to rich Triple-layered Mint Brownies, spread with creamy icing and glazed with chocolate. You can cut the bars to the size we suggest, or make them smaller, for daintier bites at a dessert buffet or tea party.

Tutti Frutti Oat Bars

Apple juice and three kinds of dried fruit—raisins, apricots, and dates—go into the filling for these oat-topped treats. Chewy and not too sweet, they're a nice addition to a cookie tray.

- ½ cup (¼ lb.) butter or margarine, at room temperature
- 1 cup firmly packed brown sugar
- 1½ cups all-purpose flour
- ½ teaspoon **each** baking soda and salt
- 1½ cups rolled oats
- 2 tablespoons water
  Fruit Filling (recipe follows)

In large bowl of an electric mixer, beat butter and sugar until creamy. In another bowl, stir together flour, baking soda, and salt; gradually add to butter mixture, blending thoroughly. Add oats and water and mix until well combined and crumbly.

Pat half the crumb mixture firmly into a greased 9- by 13-inch baking pan. Spread with cooled filling. Spoon remaining crumb mixture evenly over filling; pat down firmly. Bake in a 350° oven until lightly browned (about 35 minutes). Let cool in pan on a rack, then cut into 1½- by 2½-inch bars. Store covered. Makes about 2½ dozen.

Fruit Filling. In a small pan, combine ¼ cup **sugar** and 1 tablespoon **cornstarch**. Stir in 1 cup **unsweetened apple juice**, 1 teaspoon grated **lemon peel**, 1 tablespoon **lemon juice**, 1 cup **raisins**, and ½ cup *each* finely chopped, lightly packed **dried apricots** and lightly packed snipped **pitted dates**. Cook over medium heat, stirring, until mixture boils and thickens; let cool.

Scottish Shortbread
(Pictured on facing page)

If you're asked to take cookies along to a small holiday gathering, you're certain to please with Scottish Shortbread, a butter-rich cookie of delightful simplicity. Or try our ginger variation, enlivened with crystallized ginger as well as the ground spice.

- 1¼ cups all-purpose flour
- 3 tablespoons cornstarch
- ¼ cup sugar
- ½ cup (¼ lb.) firm butter, cut into pieces
  Sugar

In a bowl, stir together flour, cornstarch, and the ¼ cup sugar. Rub in butter with your fingers until mixture is very crumbly and no large particles remain. With your hands, gather mixture into a ball; place in an ungreased 8- or 9-inch round baking pan with a removable bottom, or in a 9-inch springform pan. Firmly press out dough into an even layer.

With the tines of a fork, make impressions around edge of dough; then prick surface evenly. Bake in a 325° oven until pale golden brown (about 40 minutes). Remove from oven and, while hot, cut with a sharp knife into 8 to 12 wedges. Sprinkle with about 1 tablespoon sugar. Let cool completely; then remove sides of pan and lift out cookies. Store airtight. Makes 8 to 12.

Ginger Shortbread

Follow directions for **Scottish Shortbread**, but substitute ½ teaspoon **ground ginger** for cornstarch. After rubbing in butter, stir in 2 tablespoons minced **crystallized ginger**.

Persimmon Bars

These soft, spicy bars, spread with a tangy glaze, are just about perfect for any festive holiday occasion. When preparing the persimmon purée, be sure to use Hachiya-type persimmons—the kind that turn very soft as they ripen. You'll recognize Hachiya persimmons by their pointed tips.

- 1 cup persimmon purée (directions follow)
- 1 teaspoon baking soda
- 1 large egg
- 1 cup sugar
- ½ cup salad oil
- 1 package (8 oz.) pitted dates, finely snipped
- 1¾ cups all-purpose flour
- 1 teaspoon **each** salt, ground cinnamon, and ground nutmeg
- ¼ teaspoon ground cloves
- 1 cup chopped walnuts or pecans
  Lemon Glaze (recipe follows)

Prepare persimmon purée; measure out 1 cup and stir in baking soda. Set aside. In a large bowl, lightly beat egg; then stir in sugar, oil, and dates.

An enduring tradition in Scotland, *rich, buttery Scottish Shortbread (facing page) is an irresistible Christmas treat.*

In another bowl, stir together flour, salt, cinnamon, nutmeg, and cloves; add to date mixture alternately with persimmon mixture, stirring just until blended. Stir in walnuts. Spread batter evenly in a lightly greased, flour-dusted rimmed 10- by 15-inch baking pan. Bake in a 350° oven until top is lightly browned and a wooden pick inserted in center comes out clean (about 25 minutes).

Let cool in pan on a rack for 5 minutes, then spread with Lemon Glaze. Let cool completely; cut into 2- by 2½-inch bars. Store covered. Makes 2½ dozen.

Persimmon purée. You'll need fully ripe **Hachiya-type persimmons**— pulp should be soft and jellylike. Cut fruits in half and scoop out pulp with a spoon. Discard skin, seeds, and stem. In a blender or food processor, whirl pulp, a portion at a time, until smooth (you'll need 2 or 3 medium-

size persimmons for 1 cup purée). For each cup purée, thoroughly stir in 1½ teaspoons **lemon juice**. To store, freeze in 1-cup batches in rigid containers; thaw, covered, at room temperature.

Lemon Glaze. In a small bowl, stir together 1 cup **powdered sugar** and 2 tablespoons **lemon juice** until smooth.

Triple-layered Mint Brownies

Extravagance is allowed at Christmas time—and that's all the excuse you need to make these devastatingly rich treats. A thin, nut-laden brownie is topped with creamy mint frosting, then covered with dark chocolate.

    2   ounces unsweetened
        chocolate
    3/4 cup (3/8 lb.) butter or
        margarine
    1   large egg
    1/2 cup granulated sugar
    1/4 cup all-purpose flour
    1   cup chopped almonds
        or pecans
    2   cups powdered sugar
    1/2 teaspoon vanilla
    1   teaspoon mint extract
    2   to 3 tablespoons
        whipping cream
        Red or green food color
        (optional)

For the first layer, place 1 ounce of the chocolate and 1/4 cup of the butter in the top of a double boiler over simmering water (or in a small pan over lowest possible heat). Stir until melted.

In a small bowl, beat egg and granulated sugar, then gradually beat in chocolate mixture. Stir in flour and almonds. Spread batter evenly in a lightly greased 9-inch square baking pan; bake in a 350° oven until brownie feels dry on top (20 to 25 minutes). Let cool completely in pan on a rack.

For the second layer, place 1/4 cup of the butter, powdered sugar, vanilla, and mint extract in small bowl of an electric mixer. Beat together; then beat in enough cream to make frosting spreadable. Tint with food color, if desired. Spread evenly over cooled brownie.

For the third layer, combine remaining 1 ounce chocolate and remaining 1/4 cup butter in the top of a double boiler over simmering water (or in a small pan over lowest possible heat). Stir until melted. Drizzle over frosting layer; tilt pan so chocolate covers surface evenly. Refrigerate until chocolate is hardened (about 15 minutes). Cut into 2 1/4-inch squares. Store, covered, in refrigerator. Makes 16.

Buttery Cookie Brittle

This delectable confection—part cookie, part candy—is studded with bits of almond brickle. You bake it in a single sheet, then break it into irregular chunks to serve.

    1/2 cup (1/4 lb.) butter or
        margarine, at room
        temperature
    3/4 teaspoon vanilla
    1   cup all-purpose flour
    1/2 cup sugar
    1   package (6 oz.) almond
        brickle bits

In large bowl of an electric mixer, beat butter and vanilla until creamy. Blend in flour and sugar, then stir in brickle bits (mixture will be quite crumbly).

Spread mixture evenly over bottom of an ungreased 9- by 13-inch baking pan. Lay a piece of wax paper on top and press firmly to pack crumbs evenly. Discard paper.

Bake in a 375° oven until golden around edges (15 to 20 minutes). Let brittle cool in pan on a rack for 10 minutes; then loosen with a wide spatula, turn out onto rack, and let cool completely. Break into pieces. Store airtight for up to 2 days; freeze for longer storage. Makes about 3 dozen 1 1/2- by 2-inch chunks.

English Toffee Squares

When you need a dessert for a large gathering, you'll appreciate this recipe. With little effort, you can produce five to six dozen delicious and easily portable toffee-flavored bar cookies.

    1   cup (1/2 lb.) butter or
        margarine, at room
        temperature
    1   cup sugar
    1   large egg
    2   cups all-purpose flour
    1   teaspoon ground
        cinnamon
    1   cup chopped pecans or
        walnuts

In large bowl of an electric mixer, beat butter and sugar until creamy. Separate egg. Beat yolk into butter mixture; cover and reserve white.

In another bowl, stir together flour and cinnamon; add to butter mixture, using your hands if necessary to blend thoroughly.

With your hands, spread dough evenly over bottom of a greased rimmed 10- by 15-inch baking pan. Beat egg white lightly, then brush over dough to cover evenly. Sprinkle pecans over top; press in lightly.

Bake in a 275° oven until firm when lightly touched (about 1 hour). While still hot, cut into about 1 1/2-inch squares. Let cool in pan on a rack. Store airtight. Makes 5 to 6 dozen.

Icebox Cookies

If you want to produce fresh-baked cookies any time, at a moment's notice, icebox cookies are for you. Make the dough in advance and store it in refrigerator or freezer; when unexpected holiday guests arrive, you can bake up teatime accompaniments or take-home treats in no time. For next-door neighbors and nearby friends, you might even consider giving rolls of the unbaked dough, plus the recipe and baking instructions.

Poppy Seed Nut Slices

Hazelnuts and poppy seeds team up to give these crunchy little cookies their distinctive flavor.

    1   cup (½ lb.) butter or
        margarine, at room
        temperature
    1   cup sugar
    1   large egg
    1   teaspoon vanilla
    2½ cups all-purpose flour
    ⅓   cup poppy seeds
    ½   teaspoon ground
        cinnamon
    ¼   teaspoon **each** salt and
        ground ginger
    1½ cups coarsely chopped
        hazelnuts

In large bowl of an electric mixer, beat butter and sugar until creamy; beat in egg and vanilla. In another bowl, stir together flour, poppy seeds, cinnamon, salt, and ginger; gradually add to butter mixture, blending thoroughly. Add hazelnuts, mixing with your hands if necessary to distribute nuts evenly. Shape dough into 2 or 3 rolls, each 1½ inches in diameter; wrap in wax paper and refrigerate until firm

(at least 2 hours) or for up to 3 days (freeze for longer storage).

Unwrap dough. Using a sharp knife, cut into ¼-inch-thick slices; place slices about 1 inch apart on ungreased baking sheets. Bake in a 350° oven until edges are golden (12 to 15 minutes). Transfer to racks and let cool. Store airtight. Makes about 7 dozen.

Spiced Almond Thins

Sour cream, brown sugar, cinnamon, and nutmeg combine in a wafer with a spicy, old-fashioned flavor that's just right for the season. Crisp bits of almond give the cookies a pebbly appearance.

    1   cup (½ lb.) butter or
        margarine, at room
        temperature
    1   cup firmly packed brown
        sugar
    2   cups all-purpose flour
    2   teaspoons ground
        cinnamon
    ½   teaspoon ground
        nutmeg
    ¼   teaspoon baking soda
    ¼   cup sour cream
    ½   cup slivered almonds

In large bowl of an electric mixer, beat butter and sugar until creamy. In another bowl, stir together flour, cinnamon, and nutmeg. Stir baking soda into sour cream; add to butter mixture alternately with flour mixture, blending thoroughly. Stir in almonds until well combined. Shape dough into a 2½-inch-thick rectangular log; wrap in wax paper and refrigerate until firm (at least 2 hours) or for up to 3 days (freeze for longer storage).

Unwrap dough. Using a sharp knife, cut into ⅛-inch-thick slices; place slices about 1 inch apart on ungreased baking sheets. Bake in a 350° oven until golden brown (about 10 minutes). Let cool for about a minute on baking sheets, then transfer to racks and let cool completely. Store airtight. Makes about 5 dozen.

French Butter Wafers

Fragile butter wafers, accented only with vanilla, provide an elegant, simple counterpoint to extra-rich holiday fare. (Since butter is responsible for much of the cookies' delicate flavor, it's best not to substitute margarine in this recipe.)

    1   cup (½ lb.) butter, at
        room temperature
    1¼ cups powdered sugar
    1   large egg
    1   teaspoon vanilla
    2   cups all-purpose flour
    1   teaspoon **each** baking
        soda and cream of tartar
    ⅛   teaspoon salt

In large bowl of an electric mixer, beat butter until creamy. Beat in sugar; add egg and vanilla and beat well. In another bowl, stir together flour, baking soda, cream of tartar, and salt; gradually add to butter mixture, blending thoroughly. Shape dough into a roll 1½ inches in diameter; wrap in wax paper and refrigerate until firm (at least 2 hours) or for up to 3 days (freeze for longer storage).

Unwrap dough. Using a sharp knife, cut into ⅜-inch-thick slices; place slices 2 inches apart on ungreased baking sheets. Bake in a 350° oven until golden (10 to 12 minutes). Let cool on baking sheets for about a minute, then transfer to racks and let cool completely. Store airtight. Makes about 4 dozen.

Black & White Squares
(Pictured below)

Jaunty stripes of vanilla- and chocolate-flavored dough give these little squares a festive appearance.

- ½ cup (¼ lb.) butter or margarine, at room temperature
- ½ cup sugar
- 1 large egg yolk
- 1½ cups all-purpose flour
- 1½ teaspoons baking powder
- ⅛ teaspoon salt
- 3 tablespoons milk
- ½ teaspoon vanilla
- 1 ounce unsweetened chocolate

In large bowl of an electric mixer, beat butter and sugar until creamy; beat in egg yolk. In another bowl, stir together flour, baking powder, and salt. In a small cup, combine milk and vanilla. Add dry ingredients to butter mixture alternately with milk mixture, blending thoroughly after each addition.

In the top of a double boiler over simmering water or in a small pan over lowest possible heat, melt chocolate, stirring constantly; let cool slightly. Divide dough in half; take 1 tablespoon dough from one half and add it to the other half. Stir chocolate into smaller portion of dough, blending until well combined.

Shape each portion of dough into a roll 1½ inches in diameter. Wrap each in wax paper; flatten sides to make square logs. Refrigerate until firm (at least 2 hours) or for up to 3 days (freeze for longer storage).

Unwrap dough. Using a sharp knife, slice each log lengthwise into fourths. Then reassemble logs, using 2 dark slices and 2 light slices for each, alternating colors to make stripes. Gently press layers together.

Cut logs crosswise into ⅛-inch-thick slices (if layers start to separate, refrigerate until dough is firmer). Place slices about 1 inch apart on greased baking sheets. Bake in a 350° oven until light golden (about 10 minutes). Transfer to racks and let cool. Store airtight. Makes about 4 dozen.

Boldly striped Black & White Squares are fun and easy to make; you form dark and light-colored logs, then cut and stack to create a pattern.

Quick Breads

Top choice for snacking throughout the year, quick breads are always popular Christmas gifts from your kitchen—and it's no wonder. They're easy to make, delicious to eat, and supremely simple to package. Just bake the loaves in foil pans; cool them right in the pans, wrap in plastic wrap, and decorate as you like. Most supermarkets sell foil loaf pans in various sizes; during the holidays, you'll sometimes find them in gold, red, or green as well as the usual silver.

Eggnog Almond Tea Loaf

When the Christmas spirit moves you, try this rich quick bread made with eggnog. Enjoy it at home, or give it as a gift—either way, it spreads holiday cheer.

- 1 cup chopped blanched almonds
- 2½ cups all-purpose flour
- ¾ cup sugar
- 3½ teaspoons baking powder
- 1 teaspoon salt
- ½ teaspoon **each** ground nutmeg and grated lemon peel
- 1 large egg
- 3 tablespoons salad oil
- 1¼ cups commercial eggnog

Spread almonds in a shallow baking pan and toast in a 350° oven until golden (about 8 minutes), stirring frequently. In a large bowl, stir together flour, sugar, baking powder, salt, nutmeg, lemon peel, and toasted almonds. In a small bowl, lightly beat egg, then beat in oil and eggnog. Add liquid mixture to flour mixture and stir just until well blended. Pour batter into a greased, flour-dusted 5- by 9-inch loaf pan (or three 3½- by 5-inch pans).

Bake in a 350° oven until a wooden pick inserted in center of bread comes out clean (about 1 hour for large loaf, 40 minutes for small loaves). Let cool in pan on a rack for 10 minutes, then turn out onto rack and let cool completely. Makes 1 large loaf or 3 small loaves.

Glazed Lemon Bread

Here's an old-fashioned favorite to enjoy in any season. While it's hot from the oven, you poke it with a skewer until it's full of holes, then drizzle it with a sweet, lemony glaze. The cooled bread is easy to slice and has a fine, even texture, much like pound cake.

- 1½ cups all-purpose flour
- 1 cup sugar
- 1 teaspoon baking powder
- ½ teaspoon salt
- 2 large eggs
- ½ cup **each** milk and salad oil
- 1½ teaspoons grated lemon peel
  Lemon Glaze (recipe follows)

In a large bowl, stir together flour, sugar, baking powder, and salt. In a small bowl, lightly beat eggs, then beat in milk, oil, and lemon peel. Add liquid mixture to flour mixture and stir just until blended.

Pour batter into a greased, flour-dusted 5- by 9-inch loaf pan. Bake in a 350° oven until a wooden pick inserted in center comes out clean (40 to 45 minutes).

When bread is done, use a long wooden skewer to poke numerous holes all the way to bottom of loaf. Drizzle hot Lemon Glaze over top so that it slowly soaks into bread. Let bread cool in pan on a rack for about 15 minutes; then turn out onto rack and let cool completely. Makes 1 loaf.

Lemon Glaze. In a small pan, combine 4½ tablespoons **lemon juice** and ⅓ cup **sugar**. Stir over medium heat until sugar is dissolved.

Date-Nut Loaf

Like fruitcake, this loaf is rich tasting, satisfying, and loaded with fruit—dates, golden raisins, and walnuts. If you like, spread each dark, sweet slice with cream cheese.

- 1¼ cups all-purpose flour
- 1 teaspoon **each** baking powder and baking soda
- ½ cup sugar
- ¼ teaspoon salt
- ½ teaspoon ground cinnamon
- 1 package (8 oz.) pitted dates, snipped
- ½ cup **each** golden raisins and chopped walnuts
- 2 tablespoons butter or margarine
- ½ teaspoon vanilla
- 1 cup hot water
- 1 large egg, lightly beaten

In a large bowl, stir together flour, baking powder, baking soda, sugar, salt, cinnamon, dates, raisins, and walnuts until thoroughly blended. In another bowl, stir together butter, vanilla, and hot water until butter is melted; then stir in egg. Pour butter mixture into dry ingredients and stir just until well blended. Pour batter into a greased 4½- by 8½-inch loaf pan.

Bake in a 325° oven until bread begins to pull away from sides of pan and a wooden pick inserted in center comes out clean—about 1 hour and 25 minutes. (Or bake for 1 hour in a 5- by 9-inch pan, or 45 minutes in two 3⅜- by 7⅜-inch pans.) Let cool in pan on a rack for 10 minutes; then turn out onto rack and let cool completely. Makes 1 large loaf or 2 small loaves.

Panettone

Traditional Milanese *panettone* is a yeast bread, but this quick version is every bit as delicious. We suggest baking it in a brown paper bag, but you can certainly use a panettone mold if you have one.

 1 *large egg*
 2 *large egg yolks*
 ¾ *cup sugar*
 ½ *cup (¼ lb.) butter or margarine, melted and cooled*
 1 *teaspoon grated lemon peel*
 1 *teaspoon **each** anise seeds and anise extract*
 ¼ *cup **each** pine nuts, raisins, and coarsely chopped mixed candied fruit*
2⅔ *cups all-purpose flour*
 2 *teaspoons baking powder*
 ½ *teaspoon salt*
 1 *cup milk*

In large bowl of an electric mixer, beat egg, egg yolks, and sugar until thick and lemon-colored. Beat in butter; then add lemon peel, anise seeds, anise extract, pine nuts, raisins, and candied fruit. In another bowl, stir together flour, baking powder, and salt. Blend half the dry ingredients into egg mixture. Stir in half the milk; add remaining dry ingredients and mix well. Blend in remaining milk.

Fold down top of a paper bag (one that measures 3½ by 6 inches on the bottom) to form a cuff so bag stands about 4 inches high. Butter inside of bag generously, set on a baking sheet, and pour in batter. (Or use a greased, flour-dusted panettone mold approximately 6 inches in diameter and 4 inches deep.)

Bake in a 325° oven until bread is well browned on top and a wooden skewer inserted in center comes out clean. To serve hot, tear off paper bag and cut bread into wedges. To serve cold, wrap bread (still in bag) in a cloth, then in foil, and let cool completely to mellow the flavors. Makes 1 loaf.

Mincemeat Bread
(Pictured on facing page)

Baked in a fluted tube pan, this spicy, pretty bread is delightful any time of day. Try it sliced thin and buttered, with tea or a hot fruit punch; or toast thicker slices for a holiday breakfast.

 ½ *cup (¼ lb.) butter or margarine, at room temperature*
 1 *cup sugar*
 3 *large eggs*
 2 *cups all-purpose flour*
 1 *tablespoon baking powder*
 ½ *teaspoon **each** salt and ground cinnamon*
1½ *cups prepared mincemeat*
 ¾ *cup chopped nuts*

In large bowl of an electric mixer, beat butter and sugar until creamy. Add eggs, 1 at a time, beating well after each addition; continue to beat until mixture is fluffy and pale yellow. In another bowl, stir together flour, baking powder, salt, and cinnamon. Add dry ingredients to creamed mixture alternately with mincemeat, mixing until thoroughly blended. Stir in nuts.

Spread batter in a generously greased, flour-dusted 8-cup fluted tube pan (or in a lightly greased, flour-dusted 5- by 9-inch loaf pan). Bake in a 350° oven until bread is lightly browned on top and a wooden pick inserted in center comes out clean (50 to 55 minutes for tube pan, about 1 hour for loaf pan). Loosen bread from pan and let cool on a rack for 10 minutes; then turn out onto rack and let cool completely. Makes 1 loaf.

Quick Orange Loaves
(Pictured on facing page)

Flecks of fresh orange add color and tangy flavor to a cinnamon-spiced nut bread. The recipe makes two plump loaves—one to enjoy right away, one to freeze or give to friends.

  About 4 large oranges
 3 *cups all-purpose flour*
 1 *teaspoon **each** salt and baking soda*
 ½ *teaspoon baking powder*
 2 *teaspoons ground cinnamon*
 1 *cup chopped nuts*
 3 *large eggs*
1½ *cups sugar*
 1 *cup salad oil*
 1 *teaspoon vanilla*

Grate 1 tablespoon orange peel. Then cut off and discard remaining peel and all white membrane from oranges. Pick out seeds; finely chop enough of the pulp to make 2 cups. In a small bowl, combine the 2 cups pulp and grated peel; set aside. In another bowl, stir together flour, salt, baking soda, baking powder, cinnamon, and nuts; set aside.

In a medium-size bowl, lightly beat eggs. Add sugar and oil and stir until blended. Stir in vanilla and orange mixture. Add flour mixture all at once and stir just until evenly moistened. Then divide batter evenly between 2 greased, flour-dusted 4½- by 8½-inch loaf pans.

Bake in a 350° oven until a wooden pick inserted in center of bread comes out clean (50 to 60 minutes). Let cool in pans on a rack for 10 minutes, then turn out onto rack and let cool completely. Wrap airtight and let stand for a day before slicing; or refrigerate for up to a week (freeze for longer storage). Makes 2 loaves.

Poppy Seed Loaf

Crunchy poppy seeds give an exciting burst of flavor to this mellow, moist tea bread. It's especially tasty when paired with our lemon-accented apricot spread; for gift giving, you might package the spread in a pretty crock or small plastic tub.

- ¼ cup (⅛ lb.) *butter or margarine, at room temperature*
- 1 cup sugar
- 2 large eggs
- 1 teaspoon grated orange peel
- 2 cups all-purpose flour
- 2½ teaspoons baking powder
- ½ teaspoon salt
- ¼ teaspoon ground nutmeg
- 1 cup milk
- ⅓ cup poppy seeds
- ½ cup chopped nuts
- ½ cup golden raisins (optional)

  Tangy Apricot Spread (recipe follows)

Beat together butter and sugar until creamy; add eggs, 1 at a time, beating well after each addition. Mix in orange peel. In another bowl, stir together flour, baking powder, salt, and nutmeg until thoroughly blended. Add flour mixture to creamed mixture alternately with milk, stirring until well blended; then stir in poppy seeds, nuts, and raisins, if desired. Turn batter into a well-greased, flour-dusted 5- by 9-inch loaf pan.

Bake in a 350° oven until bread begins to pull away from sides of pan and a wooden pick inserted in center comes out clean (about 1 hour and 10 minutes). Let cool in pan on a rack for 10 minutes, then turn out onto rack and let cool completely. Offer Tangy Apricot Spread with bread. Makes 1 loaf.

Tangy Apricot Spread. Beat together ½ cup (¼ lb.) **butter** or margarine (at room temperature), ¼ cup **apricot jam**, 1 teaspoon grated **lemon peel**, and 1 tablespoon **lemon juice**.

*A **tempting array** of holiday sweet breads includes (clockwise from top) Quick Orange Loaf (facing page), Dresden-style Stollen (page 38), Anise Bread (page 35), and Mincemeat Bread (facing page).*

Cranberry-Nut Bread
(Pictured on page 1)

Celebrate the holidays with this refreshingly tart bread, studded with bright red cranberries.

- 2 cups all-purpose flour
- ½ cup sugar
- 1½ teaspoons baking powder
- ½ teaspoon **each** salt and baking soda
- 1 egg, beaten
- 10 tablespoons orange juice
- ¼ cup (⅛ lb.) butter or margarine, melted and cooled
- 1 cup fresh or frozen cranberries, halved
- ½ cup coarsely chopped walnuts or pecans

In a large bowl, stir together flour, sugar, baking powder, salt, and baking soda until well blended. Make a well in center of flour mixture; add egg, orange juice, and butter. Stir just until dry ingredients are moistened. Stir in cranberries and walnuts. Pour batter into a greased, flour-dusted 5- by 9-inch loaf pan (or three 3½- by 5-inch loaf pans).

Bake in a 350° oven until bread is golden brown on top and a wooden pick inserted in center comes out clean (about 45 minutes for large loaf, 30 minutes for small loaves). Let cool in pan on a rack for 5 minutes; then turn out onto rack and let cool completely. Wrap airtight; store at room temperature for up to 2 days or freeze for up to 1 month. Makes 1 large loaf or 3 small loaves.

Yeast Breads

In almost every country, special sweet yeast breads are a holiday tradition. We present some of these favorites here—fruited German *stollen*, lemon-glazed Swedish *kardemummakrans*, and more. Our collection includes newer recipes, too, like plump Golden Teddy Bear Breads and little "surprise packages" filled with sweet or savory cheese. Any one would be a wonderful centerpiece for brunch or breakfast, or a warm and thoughtful gift for friends.

Part of what makes all these breads so special is imaginative shaping: some are braided, others formed into wreaths or pretzels or snowflakes. There's even an elegant Christmas tree, with curling branches to decorate with glowing candied cherries.

Golden Teddy Bear Breads
(Pictured on page 4)

Golden, charming, and sweetly scented, these teddy bear breads will entice even a Grinch on Christmas morning. The rich egg breads can be frozen, so you can bake the bears ahead if you like.

- 1 package active dry yeast
- 1/4 cup warm water (about 110°F)
- 1/2 cup (1/4 lb.) butter or margarine, at room temperature
- 1/2 cup sugar
- 2 tablespoons vanilla
- 1/3 cup warm milk (about 110°F)
- 1/2 teaspoon salt
- 5 large eggs
  About 4 3/4 cups all-purpose flour
- 1 large egg beaten with 1 tablespoon milk

In large bowl of an electric mixer, sprinkle yeast over warm water and let stand for about 5 minutes to soften. Stir in butter, sugar, vanilla, milk, salt, and the 5 eggs; beat until combined. Stir in 3 cups of the flour; beat on high speed until smooth and stretchy (about 6 minutes). Add 1 3/4 cups more flour. *If using a dough hook,* beat on high speed until dough pulls cleanly from bowl sides. *To mix by hand,* stir with a heavy spoon until flour is incorporated.

Cover dough and let rise in a warm place until doubled—about 1 hour. (Or refrigerate until doubled —18 to 24 hours.)

Scrape dough out onto a lightly floured board and knead briefly to release air, adding more flour as needed to prevent sticking. Cut dough into 4 equal pieces; cover until ready to shape.

For each bear, divide 1 dough quarter into these portions: 3 tablespoons for arms, 3 tablespoons for legs, 1/2 cup for body, about 1/4 cup for head, and 1 to 1 1/2 tablespoons for ears, face features, and belly button.

Follow picture below as you shape bear; each shaped piece should be about 1/2 inch thick. Roll arm and leg portions into 8-inch-long ropes. Shape into arcs as shown on a greased 12- by 15-inch baking sheet, spacing arcs 1 inch apart at their centers. Press center 3 inches of arcs, then brush flattened portions with egg-milk mixture.

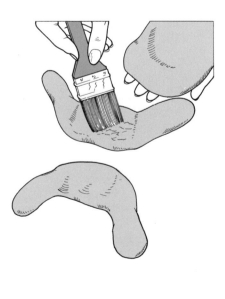

Shape body dough into an oval 5 inches long, gently pulling top surface toward underside to make smooth. Place body on flattened part of arcs. Press and tuck bottom of trunk underneath arc to secure. If necessary, pull arms and legs to make each 2 1/2 inches long.

Shape head into a ball, pulling top surface toward underside to make smooth. Press into a 2 1/2-inch-diameter circle. Press top 1/2 inch of body to flatten; brush with egg-milk mixture. Place head on baking sheet so it overlaps flat part of body; press to seal.

Shape 2/3 of remaining dough into 2 ears. Flatten 2 spots on top sides of head, about 1/4 inch in; brush with egg-milk mixture. Press ears in place.

Roll remaining dough into 4 or 5 balls: 2 for eyes, 1 for belly button, 1 for nose, and 1 for snout, if desired. (Make nose and snout pieces slightly bigger.) With a finger, poke small holes in bear for dough pieces. Brush holes with egg-milk mixture. Place dough in holes.

Loosely cover shaped bears with plastic wrap and let rise in a warm place until puffy (25 to 30 minutes). Gently brush with egg-milk mixture. Bake in a 350° oven until golden (16 to 18 minutes). If baking 2 bears at a time in 1 oven, switch position of baking sheets halfway through baking.

Let bears cool on baking sheets for 10 minutes, then transfer to a rack. Serve warm or cool. If made ahead, wrap airtight and freeze for up to 1 month. Makes 4 bear breads (3/4 lb. each); each makes 2 or 3 servings.

Miniature Breads

Tiny braided loaves and rings made from an egg-rich yeast dough are pleasing gifts—and a pretty offering for a Christmas or New Year's breakfast.

    1   package active dry yeast
    1¼   cups warm water
         (about 110°F)
    1   teaspoon salt
    ¼   cup **each** sugar and
         salad oil
    2   large eggs, lightly beaten
    2   or 3 drops yellow food
         color (optional)
         About 5 cups all-purpose
         flour
    1   large egg yolk beaten
         with 1 tablespoon water
         About 1 tablespoon
         sesame or poppy seeds
         (optional)

In a large bowl, sprinkle yeast over warm water and let stand for about 5 minutes to soften. Stir in salt, sugar, oil, eggs, and food color (if used). Add 2½ cups of the flour and beat until batter is smooth.

If using a dough hook, gradually beat in 2 cups more flour, beating between additions until dough pulls away from bowl in stretchy strands. *If mixing by hand,* slowly add 2 cups more flour, beating constantly with a heavy spoon until dough is smooth and stretchy.

Scrape dough out onto a board sprinkled with about ¼ cup more flour; knead until smooth and satiny (about 15 minutes), adding more flour as needed to prevent sticking. Place dough in a greased bowl, turn over to grease top, cover, and let rise in a warm place until doubled (1¼ hours).

Punch dough down and knead briefly on floured board to release air, then divide in half. Roll each half into a 24-inch log, then cut each log into 15 equal pieces. Working with 3 pieces at a time (keep remaining dough covered with plastic wrap),

roll each into a 24-inch rope. Pinch ropes together at one end and braid to a 21-inch length.

To make loaves, cut braid into 3-inch lengths, pinching both ends. For rings, cut braid into 7-inch lengths, pinching ends together to form a circle. Place breads 2 inches apart on greased baking sheets. Cover and let rise in a warm place until dough is smooth and puffy (about 15 minutes).

When breads are ready to bake, lightly brush with egg yolk mixture. Sprinkle with sesame or poppy seeds, if desired. Bake in a 400° oven until light golden brown (about 12 minutes). Makes 70 loaves or 30 rings.

Swedish Kardemummakrans

(Pictured on pages 1 and 39)

Flavored with aromatic cardamom, our braided Swedish wreaths can be made ahead, then reheated for a special breakfast treat. Since cutting tends to squash this tender bread, it's best to pull it apart to serve.

    1   package active dry yeast
    ¼   cup warm water
         (about 110°F)
    2½   cups warm milk
         (about 110°F)
    ¾   cup (⅜ lb.) butter or
         margarine, melted and
         cooled
    1   large egg
    ½   teaspoon salt
    1   cup sugar
    1½   teaspoons ground
         cardamom
         About 8 cups all-purpose
         flour
         Lemon Icing
         (recipe follows)
         Red or green candied
         cherries, halved
         (optional)

In a large bowl, sprinkle yeast over warm water and let stand for about 5 minutes to soften. Stir in milk, butter, egg, salt, sugar, and cardamom until blended.

With a heavy spoon, stir in 7 cups of the flour or enough to form a stiff dough. Scrape dough out onto a lightly floured board and knead until smooth and elastic (about 10 minutes), adding more flour as needed to prevent sticking. Place dough in a greased bowl, turn over to grease top, cover, and let rise in a warm place until almost doubled (1½ to 2 hours).

Punch dough down and knead briefly on a floured board to release air. Then divide into 6 equal portions; roll each into a rope about 24 inches long. Place 3 ropes on a greased baking sheet, pinch tops together, and braid loosely. Form braid into a ring, pinching ends together. Repeat to make a second braided wreath. Cover and let rise in a warm place until almost doubled (about 40 minutes).

Bake in a 350° oven until loaves are medium brown (35 to 40 minutes). Transfer loaves to a rack and let cool for 10 minutes, then serve warm. Or, if made ahead, let cool completely, then wrap airtight and freeze. Thaw unwrapped. To reheat, wrap in foil and heat in a 350° oven for about 20 minutes.

To serve, spoon half the Lemon Icing around top of each warm wreath, letting it drizzle down sides. Decorate with cherries, if desired. Makes 2 loaves.

Lemon Icing. Combine 2 cups **powdered sugar**, ¼ cup **milk**, and 1 teaspoon **lemon extract**. Stir until smooth.

Cut-and-Slash Loaves
(Pictured on facing page)

Two easy techniques—cut and slash—bring holiday designs to a simple sweet bread. Knife cuts form a simple round or triangle into a snowflake, wreath, or tree; slashes made with a razor blade add decorative touches.

> 1 package active dry yeast
> 1/4 cup warm water (about 110°F)
> 3/4 cup warm milk (about 110°F)
> 1/2 cup (1/4 lb.) butter or margarine, melted and cooled
> 1/2 cup sugar
> 1/2 teaspoon salt
> 1 teaspoon grated lemon peel
> 3 large eggs
> 4 1/4 to 4 1/2 cups all-purpose flour

In a large bowl, sprinkle yeast over warm water and let stand for about 5 minutes to soften. Mix in milk, butter, sugar, salt, lemon peel, 2 of the eggs, and 2 cups of the flour; stir to blend, then beat until smooth.

If using a dough hook, add 2 1/4 cups more flour and beat until dough pulls from bowl sides and feels only slightly sticky; add more flour if needed.

If mixing by hand, stir in 2 1/4 cups more flour with a heavy spoon. Then scrape dough onto a floured board and knead until smooth and satiny (10 to 15 minutes). Add more flour as needed to prevent sticking.

Place dough in a greased bowl; turn over to grease top. Cover dough

mixed by either method; let rise in a warm place until doubled (1 to 1 1/2 hours).

Punch dough down; knead briefly on a floured board to release air, then divide in half. Shape each portion, following directions below. Lightly cover with plastic wrap and let rise in a warm place until almost doubled (30 to 45 minutes). Beat remaining egg. Brush dough with egg; slash as directed below.

Bake in 350° oven until browned (25 to 30 minutes). Transfer to racks; let cool for about 10 minutes, then serve warm. Or, if made ahead, wrap airtight and freeze; thaw unwrapped. To reheat, cover loaves lightly with foil and heat in a 350° oven until warm (7 to 10 minutes). Makes 2 loaves.

Snowflake. Form 1 portion of dough into a ball. Place in center of a greased 10- by 15-inch baking sheet. Press dough into a flat 8-inch round. Make 4 equidistant 3-inch cuts toward center.

After shaped dough has risen, brush with egg. Using a razor blade, make a 3-inch slash down center of each quarter, then cut three 1 1/2- to 2-inch slashes down each side of each center slash.

Wreath. Press 1 portion of dough into an 8-inch round as described for snowflake. Poke a hole in center and pull equally from each side of hole to make a 2-inch opening in center; keep dough an even 3/4-inch thickness as you work. Cut 2- to 2 1/2-inch slanting cuts in from edge, spacing them about 3 inches apart (see photo on facing page).

After shaped dough has risen, brush with egg. Using a razor blade, cut a 3-inch slash down center of each leaf.

Tree. On a greased 10- by 15-inch baking sheet, form 1 portion of dough into a flat triangle with a 6-inch base and 9-inch sides. Make 2 1/2- to 3 1/2-inch slanting cuts along the sides, spacing them about 3 inches apart (see photo on facing page).

After shaped dough has risen, brush with egg. Using a razor blade, slash down triangle's center and cut a 2- to 3-inch-long slash down each branch.

Christmas Surprise Bread Bundles
(Pictured on page 34)

Tie bright bows around golden bread bundles, and the butter-rich dough becomes gift wrapping for the sweet or tangy cheese filling inside. You need to chill the dough for easy handling, so start a day ahead—or even weeks ahead, since the bread bundles freeze well.

> 1 package active dry yeast
> 1/4 cup warm water (about 110°F)
> 1/2 cup (1/4 lb.) butter or margarine, melted
> 1/2 cup half-and-half, light cream, or milk
> 3 tablespoons sugar (omit if using savory filling)
> 3 large eggs
> 4 to 4 1/2 cups all-purpose flour
> 1 teaspoon ground nutmeg
> 1/2 teaspoon salt
> Sweet Cheese Filling or Savory Cheese Filling (recipes follow)
> 1 large egg beaten with 1 tablespoon water

In large bowl of an electric mixer, sprinkle yeast over warm water and let stand for about 5 minutes to soften. Mix butter, half-and-half, and sugar (if used); add to yeast mixture with the 3 eggs, 2 cups of the flour, nutmeg, and salt. Stir to blend. Beat on medium speed for 2 minutes.

If using a dough hook, gradually mix in 2 cups more flour; beat on medium speed until dough pulls from bowl sides. Add 2 to 4 more tablespoons flour, if needed. Remove hook; scrape down bowl.

To mix by hand, beat in 1 3/4 cups more flour with a heavy spoon. Scrape dough out onto a board coated with about 1/4 cup flour; knead until smooth and elastic (about 10 minutes).

Place dough in a greased bowl; turn over to grease top. Cover dough

Handsome golden Cut-and-Slash Loaves (facing page), shaped as fanciful wreath, tree, and snowflake, are delightful, easy-to-make gifts.

mixed by either method and let rise in a warm place until doubled (about 1½ hours). Punch down; knead briefly, then wrap airtight and refrigerate for at least 2 hours or until next day.

Knead dough briefly on a floured board to release air, then divide into 16 equal portions. Shape each portion into a 6- to 6½-inch circle. Place equal portions (2 to 2½ tablespoons) of filling in center of each circle. Draw dough up around filling and pleat; then pinch firmly just above filling, letting top of dough flare loosely. As you finish bundles, place them 2 inches apart on greased 10- by 15-inch baking sheets; cover loosely with plastic wrap and keep cold until all dough is shaped.

Place baking sheets with covered bundles in a warm place and let rise until puffy (about 30 minutes); then uncover. To seal firmly, lightly pinch pleats together again. Brush surfaces with egg-water mixture. Bake in a 350° oven until golden brown (about 25 minutes). Serve warm or at room temperature. If made ahead, let cool completely; wrap airtight and freeze for up to 6 months. Thaw unwrapped. To reheat, set slightly apart on baking sheets and heat in a 325° oven for about 20 minutes. Makes 16 buns.

Sweet Cheese Filling. Beat together 2 large packages (8 oz. *each*)

Sweet little Christmas Surprise Bread Bundles, *gaily beribboned, make special presents from your kitchen. (Recipe begins on page 32.)*

cream cheese, at room temperature; ½ cup powdered sugar; 1 large egg; 2 teaspoons grated orange peel; and ¼ teaspoon almond extract. Stir in 1 cup raisins and ½ cup chopped candied orange peel. Use, or cover and refrigerate until next day.

Savory Cheese Filling. Beat together 1 large package (8 oz.) cream cheese, at room temperature; 8 ounces feta cheese, crumbled; 1 large egg; and 1 cup finely chopped green onions (including tops). Use, or cover and refrigerate until next day.

Vanocka

For many families, a holiday morning means a special breakfast bread. In Czechoslovakia, this might be *vanocka*—a plump and glossy braided loaf, filled with chopped candied fruit and nuts and flavored with lemon.

- 2 packages active dry yeast
- 1 cup warm water (about 110°F)

  About 5 cups all-purpose flour
- ½ cup *each* raisins and water
- 2 tablespoons rum or brandy (optional)
- 1 cup (½ lb.) butter or margarine, at room temperature
- ½ cup sugar
- 2 large eggs
- 1 teaspoon *each* salt and grated lemon peel
- ½ cup *each* chopped blanched almonds and chopped mixed candied fruit
- 1 large egg beaten with 1 tablespoon water

In a large bowl, sprinkle yeast over the 1 cup warm water and let stand for about 5 minutes to soften. Stir in 1 cup of the flour and beat until well blended. Cover and let stand in a warm place until bubbly (about 1 hour).

Meanwhile, in a small bowl, soak raisins in the ½ cup water for 1 hour. Pour off and discard water; add rum, if desired, and set aside.

In a large bowl, beat butter until creamy. Gradually add sugar, beating until light and fluffy. Add the 2 eggs, 1 at a time, beating well after each addition. Stir in salt and lemon peel. Add butter mixture to yeast mixture, stirring until blended.

Gradually beat in 2 cups more flour. Stir in raisins, almonds, and candied fruit. Gradually beat in about 1½ cups more flour or enough to make a stiff dough.

Scrape dough out onto a floured board and knead until smooth and satiny (about 10 minutes), adding more flour as needed to prevent sticking. Place dough in a greased bowl; turn over to grease top. Cover and let rise in a warm place until doubled (about 1½ hours).

Punch dough down; knead briefly on a floured board to release air. Divide into 6 equal portions and roll each into a 10-inch-long rope. For each loaf, arrange 3 ropes side by side on a greased 12- by 15-inch baking sheet. Pinch together at top and braid loosely; pinch ends together and tuck underneath. Cover and let rise in a warm place until almost doubled (30 to 40 minutes).

Brush loaves with egg mixture and bake in a 350° oven until browned (about 30 minutes). Transfer to racks to cool. Makes 2 loaves.

Anise Bread
(Pictured on page 29)

For festive occasions in northeastern New Mexico, it's a tradition to bake a sweet yeast bread with the flavor of anise. Serve this tender treat warm or toasted to enhance its spicy fragrance.

- 1 package active dry yeast
- ½ cup warm water (about 110°F)
- ½ cup warm milk (about 110°F)
- 2 tablespoons granulated sugar
- 1½ tablespoons anise seeds
- ½ cup (¼ lb.) butter or margarine, melted and cooled
- 2 large eggs
- ½ teaspoon salt
- 4½ to 5 cups all-purpose flour
- ⅔ cup firmly packed brown sugar mixed with ½ teaspoon ground cinnamon

  Sugar Glaze (recipe follows)

In a large bowl, sprinkle yeast over warm water and let stand for about 5 minutes to soften. Add milk, granulated sugar, anise seeds, 3 tablespoons of the butter, eggs, salt, and 1½ cups of the flour. Beat for about 5 minutes, then gradually beat in about 2½ cups more flour to make a soft dough.

Scrape dough out onto a floured board; knead until smooth and satiny (15 to 20 minutes), adding more flour as needed to prevent sticking. Place dough in a greased bowl; turn over to grease top. Cover and let rise in a warm place until doubled (about 1½ hours). Punch dough down, knead briefly on a lightly floured board to release air, and roll out into a 12- by 22-inch rectangle. Brush remaining 5 tablespoons butter over dough to within ½ inch of edges. Sprinkle brown sugar–cinnamon mixture evenly over butter. Starting with a long side, roll up dough tightly jelly roll style; pinch edge to seal.

Being careful not to stretch roll, place it seam side down in a greased 10-inch tube pan; pinch ends together to close circle. With a razor blade or floured sharp knife, make 7 evenly spaced slashes, ½ inch deep, on top. Cover and let rise in a warm place until almost doubled (about 45 minutes).

Bake in a 350° oven until loaf is lightly browned (50 to 60 minutes). Let cool in pan for 5 minutes; then turn out onto a rack. While bread is still warm, spoon on Sugar Glaze, letting it drizzle down sides. Makes 1 loaf.

Sugar Glaze. Blend ½ cup powdered sugar with 1 tablespoon water until smooth.

Christmas Tree Bread

With its braided trunk and glossy, elegantly curled branches, this Christmas tree is a lovely choice for brunch any time during the Yuletide season. The recipe makes three trees —two to give away and one to serve to your family.

    2   packages active dry yeast
    ½   cup warm water
        (about 110°F)
    4   large eggs, lightly beaten
    1⅔ cups evaporated milk,
        at room temperature
        Pinch of ground saffron
    1   teaspoon salt
    1½ cups sugar
        About 9 cups all-purpose
        flour
    1   cup (½ lb.) butter or
        margarine, melted and
        cooled
        Red or green candied
        cherries, halved
    1   large egg, beaten

In a very large bowl, sprinkle yeast over warm water and let stand for about 5 minutes to soften. Mix in the 4 eggs, evaporated milk, saffron, salt, and sugar. Beat until saffron is evenly distributed.

Gradually add 4½ cups of the flour, beating until dough is smooth and elastic. Stir in butter until well blended.

If using a dough hook, beat in 4 cups more flour or enough to form a stiff dough. *If mixing by hand,* beat in

4 cups more flour with a heavy spoon, mixing to make a stiff dough.

Sprinkle a board with about ½ cup more flour. Scrape dough out onto board, cover lightly, and let stand for 15 minutes. Then knead until smooth and elastic, adding more flour as needed to prevent sticking. Place dough in a greased bowl; turn over to grease top. Cover tightly with plastic wrap and refrigerate until next day.

Cut dough into 3 equal parts. To shape each tree, divide 1 part into 16 equal portions; roll each into a 12-inch strand.

Shape each tree on a greased large baking sheet as shown below. First, cut two 5-inch pieces from one 12-inch strand to form top pair of branches; curl 1 end of each of these branches and bring cut ends together at center top of tree. Reserve excess dough to use later. Use another 12-inch strand to make second pair of branches, cutting strand into two 6-inch pieces. To make succeeding pairs of branches, use 1 rope for each branch; curl 1 end and arrange branches so each curled end extends about ½ inch farther out from center of tree than the curl just above it (curls should just touch each other). Cut off excess dough at center as you form each branch.

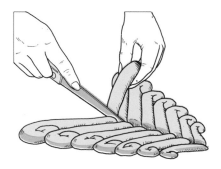

Continue making branches until you have placed 9 pairs. Then combine all excess dough scraps; use some of this dough to roll an 8-inch-long strand to fit below last pair of branches (leave ends uncurled as shown above right). Roll remaining dough to make 3 thin strands, each about 20 inches long. Braid these for trunk of tree. Press trunk in place; then press a cherry half into curl at end of each branch.

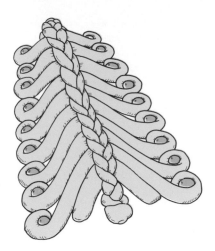

Cover bread and let rise in a warm place for 25 minutes. Brush with beaten egg; bake in a 400° oven for 10 minutes. Brush again with egg and continue to bake until bread is golden brown (15 to 20 more minutes). Makes 3 loaves.

Bohemian Christmas Braid

Much like Vanocka (page 35), this braided loaf is flavored with lemon peel and studded with almonds and fruit. The shaping is a bit different, though—this is a double braid (a smaller braid atop a larger one). Almond-flavored icing, pecan halves, and cherries provide a fancy Christmas finish.

    1   package active dry yeast
    ¼   cup warm water
        (about 110°F)
    1   cup warm milk
        (about 110°F)
    ⅓   cup sugar
    1½ teaspoons **each** salt and
        grated lemon peel
    1   teaspoon ground mace
    2   tablespoons butter or
        margarine, at room
        temperature
    1   large egg
        About 4 cups all-purpose
        flour
    ½   cup **each** raisins and
        chopped unblanched
        almonds

*Almond Icing
(recipe follows)
Pecan halves
Red candied cherries,
halved*

In large bowl of an electric mixer, sprinkle yeast over warm water and let stand for about 5 minutes to soften. Add milk, sugar, salt, lemon peel, mace, butter, egg, and 1½ cups of the flour. Beat on medium speed until smooth (about 5 minutes).

If using a dough hook, beat in about 2½ cups more flour or enough to form a soft, elastic dough. *To mix by hand,* beat in about 2½ cups more flour with a heavy spoon.

Scrape dough out of bowl and shape into a ball, then place in a greased bowl and turn over to grease top. Cover and let rise in a warm place until doubled (about 1 hour).

Stir down dough, blending in raisins and almonds. Then scrape dough out onto a board coated with about 2 tablespoons flour and knead lightly until smooth.

Divide dough into 4 equal pieces. Shape 3 pieces into smooth ropes about 16 inches long. Place ropes side by side on a greased baking sheet and braid tightly; pinch ends to seal, then tuck underneath.

Divide remaining dough into 3 pieces. Shape each into a smooth 10-inch-long rope. Braid tightly; pinch ends to seal, then tuck underneath. Lightly moisten top of large braid with water and place smaller braid on top. Cover lightly and let rise in a warm place until almost doubled (about 30 minutes).

Bake in a 350° oven until well browned (25 to 30 minutes). Transfer to a rack and let cool for about 10 minutes, then serve warm. Or, if made ahead, let cool completely, then wrap airtight and freeze; thaw unwrapped. To reheat, wrap loaf in foil and place in a 350° oven for about 20 minutes.

To serve, drizzle warm bread with icing and decorate with pecan halves and cherries. Makes 1 loaf.

Almond Icing. Stir together ¾ cup **powdered sugar**, 2 to 3 teaspoons **milk**, and ⅛ teaspoon **almond extract**.

Belgian Cramique
(Pictured on page 39)

This beautiful, golden-crusted raisin bread is made up of topknotted brioche-type rolls, arranged and baked in a wreath.

 1   cup milk
 ¼   cup (⅛ lb.) butter or
     margarine, cut into
     pieces
 ⅓   cup sugar
 1   teaspoon salt
 2   packages active dry yeast
 ½   cup warm water
     (about 110°F)
 3   large eggs
 5½ to 6 cups all-purpose
     flour
 1   cup raisins
 1   large egg yolk beaten
     with 1 tablespoon water

In a pan, combine milk, butter, sugar, and salt. Heat, stirring, to about 110°F (butter need not melt completely). In a large bowl, sprinkle yeast over warm water and let stand for about 5 minutes to soften. Stir softened yeast and eggs into milk mixture. Gradually beat in 5 cups of the flour to make a soft dough.

Add raisins and scrape dough out onto a floured board; knead until smooth and satiny (5 to 20 minutes), adding more flour as needed to prevent sticking. Place dough in a greased bowl; turn over to grease top. Cover and let rise in a warm place until doubled (about 45 minutes).

Punch dough down and knead briefly on a floured board to release air; then divide into 12 equal parts. Pinch off about ⅕ of each part and set aside to shape topknots. Shape each larger piece into a smooth ball; place, smooth side up, around edges of 2 greased 9-inch round cake pans (each pan will hold 6 balls). Shape each smaller piece into a teardrop that is smooth on top. With your finger, poke a hole in center of each large ball and insert pointed end of teardrop in hole—settle it securely or it may pop off at an angle while baking. Cover and let rise in a

warm place until almost doubled (about 45 minutes).

Brush loaves with egg yolk mixture, being careful not to let it accumulate in joints of topknots. Bake in a 350° oven until richly browned (about 45 minutes). Let cool in pans for 5 minutes, then turn out onto racks to cool completely. Makes 2 wreaths.

Swedish Letter Buns
(Lussekätter)

In Sweden during the holiday season, sweet little S-shaped rolls are typically served with the hot wine punch called *glögg*. They're made from a light, buttery dough flavored with cardamom or saffron, then adorned with raisins.

 ½   cup (¼ lb.) butter or
     margarine
 ¾   cup whipping cream
     or milk
 ⅓   cup sugar
 ½   teaspoon salt
 1   teaspoon ground
     cardamom or 1/16
     teaspoon ground saffron
 1   package active dry yeast
 ¼   cup warm water
     (about 110°F)
 1   large egg
     About 4 cups all-purpose
     flour
     About ⅓ cup raisins
 1   large egg yolk beaten
     with 1 tablespoon water

In a small pan, melt butter; remove from heat and stir in cream, sugar, salt, and cardamom. Let cool to lukewarm.

In large bowl of an electric mixer, sprinkle yeast over warm water and let stand for about 5 minutes to soften. Add cooled cream mixture, egg, and 2 cups of the flour. Mix until well blended, then beat on medium speed for 2 more minutes.

If using a dough hook, gradually beat in about 1½ cups more flour to make a stiff dough. *To mix by hand,* stir in about 1½ cups more flour with a heavy spoon; beat to make a stiff dough.

Scrape dough out onto a floured board and knead until smooth and satiny (about 10 minutes), adding more flour as needed to prevent sticking. Place dough in a greased bowl; turn over to grease top. Cover and let rise in a warm place until doubled (about 1½ hours).

Punch dough down; knead briefly on a floured board to release air. To shape rolls, divide dough into 24 equal pieces; roll each piece on a flat surface with your palm to make a rope about 9 inches long, and coil ends of each in opposite directions to form an S shape. Push a raisin deep into center of each coil.

Place rolls about 2 inches apart on 2 greased 14- by 17-inch baking sheets. Cover and let rise in a warm place until puffy and almost doubled (about 45 minutes). Brush rolls with egg yolk mixture. With racks placed in the upper and lower middle of a 375° oven, bake buns until golden brown on bottoms and lightly browned around edges (about 15 minutes; switch positions of baking sheets halfway through baking, if necessary for even browning). Makes 2 dozen rolls.

Dresden-style Stollen
(Pictured on pages 1 and 29)

There are many versions of Germany's famous *stollen;* one of the most popular is this one from Dresden. Its rich, buttery dough, studded with candied orange peel, almonds, raisins, and currants, is folded a special way to form an ellipse-shaped loaf, then dusted with powdered sugar after baking.

½   cup milk
1   cup (½ lb.) butter or margarine
½   cup granulated sugar
2   packages active dry yeast
½   cup warm water (about 110°F)
½   teaspoon salt
1   teaspoon **each** grated lemon peel and almond extract
  About 5¼ cups all-purpose flour
2   large eggs
⅓   cup finely chopped candied orange peel
½   cup **each** dark raisins, golden raisins, currants, and slivered almonds
1   large egg white beaten with 1 teaspoon water
¼   cup (⅛ lb.) butter or margarine, melted
⅓   cup powdered sugar

In a small pan, combine milk, the 1 cup butter, and granulated sugar. Set over medium-low heat and heat to scalding (120°F), stirring to dissolve sugar and melt butter. Set aside; let cool to lukewarm.

In a large bowl, sprinkle yeast over warm water and let stand for about 5 minutes to soften. Add cooled milk mixture, salt, lemon peel, almond extract, and 3 cups of the flour; beat until well blended. Add eggs, 1 at a time, beating well after each addition. Gradually stir in orange peel, raisins, currants, almonds, and 2 cups more flour.

Scrape dough out onto a floured board and knead until smooth and satiny (about 10 minutes), adding more flour as needed to prevent sticking. Place dough in a greased bowl; turn over to grease top. Cover and let rise in a warm place until doubled (about 1½ hours).

Punch dough down. Knead briefly on a floured board to release air, then divide in half. Place each portion on a lightly greased 12- by 15-inch baking sheet and shape into a 7- by 9-inch oval about ¾ inch thick. Brush surface with some of the egg white mixture. Crease each oval lengthwise, slightly off center, and fold so top edge lies about an inch back from bottom edge. Brush

evenly with remaining egg white mixture. Cover and let rise in a warm place until puffy and almost doubled (35 to 45 minutes).

Bake in a 375° oven until richly browned (about 25 minutes). Brush loaves evenly with the ¼ cup melted butter and sift powdered sugar over tops. Return to oven and bake for 3 more minutes. Transfer to racks and let cool. Makes 2 loaves.

Russian Krendl'
(Pictured on facing page)

Krendl' is a traditional birthday treat in Russia—at Christmastime, it celebrates the birth of Jesus.

2   packages active dry yeast
½   cup warm water (about 110°F)
1¼   teaspoons salt
3   tablespoons sugar
2   teaspoons vanilla
1   cup warm milk (about 110°F)
  About 6 cups all-purpose flour
6   large egg yolks, lightly beaten
½   cup (¼ lb.) plus 1 tablespoon butter or margarine, melted and cooled
½   teaspoon ground cinnamon
¼   cup sugar
⅔   cup chopped seeded canned kumquats
1   cup **each** chopped moist-pack pitted prunes and chopped dried apples
1   large egg yolk beaten with 1 tablespoon water
  Sugar Glaze (recipe follows)
¼   cup sliced almonds

In a large bowl, sprinkle yeast over warm water and let stand for about 5 minutes to soften. Add salt, the 3 tablespoons sugar, vanilla, and milk. Beat in 2 cups of the flour to make a smooth batter.

Blend in the 6 egg yolks and ½ cup of the butter, then stir in about

A selection of festive sweet breads brings Old World tradition to your holidays. From top: *Russian Krendl'* (facing page), *Swedish Kardemummakrans* (page 31), and *Belgian Cramique* (page 37).

3½ cups more flour or enough to make a soft dough. Scrape out onto a lightly floured board and knead until smooth (about 5 minutes), adding more flour as needed to prevent sticking. Place dough in a greased bowl; turn over to grease top. Cover and let rise in a warm place until doubled (about 45 minutes).

Punch dough down and knead briefly on a floured board to release air. Divide dough in half; roll each half into a 9- by 30-inch rectangle. Spread rectangles with remaining 1 tablespoon butter, dividing evenly.

Combine cinnamon and the ¼ cup sugar; sprinkle half the mixture over each rectangle. Then scatter half of the kumquats, prunes, and apples evenly over each rectangle.

To shape loaves, tightly roll up each rectangle jelly roll style, starting from a long side. Moisten edge with water and pinch seam to seal along side of roll.

Place each roll, seam side down, on a greased baking sheet; form into a modified pretzel shape by crossing 1 end over the other and tucking ends under center of roll. Flatten loaf slightly.

Cover loaves and let rise in a warm place until almost doubled (about 40 minutes). Brush with egg yolk mix-

ture and bake in a 350° oven until browned (40 to 45 minutes). Transfer to a rack; let cool for 20 minutes, then serve warm. Or, if made ahead, let cool completely; wrap airtight and freeze. To reheat, wrap frozen loaves in foil; heat in a 350° oven for 50 minutes.

To serve, brush half the glaze on each warm loaf. Immediately sprinkle with almonds. Makes 2 loaves.

Sugar Glaze. Beat together 1 tablespoon **butter** or margarine (melted), 2 tablespoons **hot water**, 1½ cups **powdered sugar**, and ¼ teaspoon grated **lemon peel** until smooth.

Cakes

To many of us, Christmas cake means only fruitcake—rich, dense loaves of wall-to-wall fruit and nuts, cut into thin slices that gleam with the gold of apricots and pineapple, the red and green of candied cherries. But other cakes shouldn't be forgotten. Dainty cheesecake miniatures, buttery pound cakes soaked with liqueur, even old-fashioned carrot cake are all worthy of a place on the holiday table. In these pages, we've selected some of our favorite Christmas cakes—some with fruit, some without, and all exceptionally good.

Liqueur Pound Cake

Rich cakes soaked in liqueur are a delightful surprise for friends during the holiday season. Because they store well unrefrigerated, they make perfect gifts to leave under the tree or to send to loved ones in distant places. The recipe makes four cakes.

1½	cups (¾ lb.) butter or margarine, at room temperature
1	pound powdered sugar
6	large eggs
1	teaspoon vanilla
2¾	cups cake flour
	Liqueur Syrup (recipe follows)

In large bowl of an electric mixer, beat butter until creamy. Sift powdered sugar; gradually add to butter, beating until mixture is light and fluffy. Add eggs, 1 at a time, beating well after each addition. Beat in vanilla. Gradually mix flour into creamed mixture.

Scrape batter evenly into four greased, flour-dusted 3½- by 7-inch loaf pans. Smooth top of batter.

Bake in a 300° oven until a wooden pick inserted in center of cake comes out clean (about 50 minutes). Let cool in pans on a rack for 5 minutes. Run a knife around edges of each pan and turn cake out; immediately return cake to pan. With a slender wooden skewer or a fork, poke 1-inch-deep holes, about ½ inch apart, all over top of cake. Immediately pour an equal amount of Liqueur Syrup over each cake. Let cool on a rack for about 30 minutes.

Remove from pans and serve; or wrap securely and store in a cool area for up to 2 weeks, in the refrigerator for up to 1 month, or in the freezer for up to 6 months. Bring to room temperature before serving. Makes 4 cakes, 4 to 6 servings each.

Liqueur Syrup. In a 2- to 3-quart pan, combine 2 cups **sugar**, ½ cup **light corn syrup**, and ¾ cup **water**. Set over medium-high heat and stir slowly until mixture comes to a simmer. Continue heating, without stirring, until mixture boils. Cover and continue to boil until sugar is dissolved and liquid is clear—about 1 minute. (If you don't cover pan and if you stir while syrup boils, crunchy sugar crystals will form in the finished cake.)

Remove from heat, uncover, and let stand until slightly cooled (about 5 minutes). Stir in 1¼ cups **rum** or almond-, hazelnut-, or orange-flavored liqueur. Use; or let cool, then cover and let stand at room temperature until next day. Makes 3½ cups.

Chocolate Liqueur Pound Cake

Follow directions for **Liqueur Pound Cake**, but decrease powdered sugar to 3 cups (12 oz.). Combine butter and sugar, then add 5 ounces **semisweet chocolate**, melted. Cakes develop a thin, crisp top crust as they bake.

Prepare **Liqueur Syrup** as directed, but decrease water to ½ cup and increase rum or liqueur to 1½ cups. Options include almond-, hazelnut-, orange-, coffee-, and chocolate-flavored liqueur. As syrup soaks through cake, top crust softens.

Carrot Cake

The best cakes are good any time—so there's no reason your friends shouldn't enjoy carrot cake during the Christmas season. Topped with a smooth cream cheese frosting and studded with nuts and pineapple, this all-year favorite is just about irresistible.

4	large eggs
1½	cups salad oil
2	cups sugar
2	cups all-purpose flour
1½	teaspoons baking soda
2	teaspoons **each** baking powder and ground cinnamon
½	teaspoon ground nutmeg
1	teaspoon salt
2	cups shredded carrots
½	cup coarsely chopped walnuts or pecans
1	can (8 oz.) crushed pineapple, drained
	Cream Cheese Frosting (recipe follows)

In a large bowl, beat eggs just until blended; add oil and sugar and beat until thoroughly mixed. In another bowl, stir together flour, baking soda, baking powder, cinnamon, nutmeg, and salt. Add to egg mixture, stirring just until blended; then mix in carrots, walnuts, and pineapple.

Pour batter into a greased, flour-dusted 9- by 13-inch baking pan or a 12-cup fluted tube or Bundt pan. Bake in a 350° oven until a wooden pick inserted in center comes out clean (45 minutes for a 9- by 13-inch pan, 55 minutes for a tube or Bundt pan).

Let cool. If you used a tube or Bundt pan, let cake cool in pan on a rack for 15 minutes; then invert onto rack and let cool completely.

Spread Cream Cheese Frosting over cooled cake. Makes 12 to 15 servings.

Cream Cheese Frosting. In small bowl of an electric mixer, combine 2 small packages (3 oz. *each*) **cream cheese**, at room temperature; 6 tablespoons **butter** or margarine, at room temperature; and 1 teaspoon grated **orange peel**. Beat until smooth. Add 1 teaspoon **vanilla** and 2 cups **powdered sugar**; beat until creamy. (Or combine all ingredients in a food processor and whirl until blended.)

Golden Apricot-Almond Fruitcake

Here's an exceptionally pretty light fruitcake, made with dried apricots, slivered almonds, and lots of golden raisins. Bake it in two large or four smaller loaves; spoon rum over the hot cakes for extra flavor, if you like.

    1½ cups dried apricots
    ⅔   cup water
    ¾   cup (⅜ lb.) butter or
        margarine, at room
        temperature
    ¾   cup sugar
    4   large eggs
    ½   teaspoon *each* salt and
        baking soda
    2   cups all-purpose flour
    1   cup *each* red candied
        cherries and slivered
        almonds
    1½ cups golden raisins
    ½   teaspoon grated
        lemon peel
    ¼   cup rum (optional)

Cut apricots into quarters. In a 1-quart pan, combine apricots and water; bring to a boil, then reduce heat and simmer, uncovered, until tender (about 2 minutes). Let cool.

In large bowl of an electric mixer, beat butter and sugar until creamy. Add eggs, 1 at a time, beating well after each addition. Stir together salt, baking soda, and 1½ cups of the flour; stir into creamed mixture. Combine cooled apricots with cherries, almonds, raisins, lemon peel, and remaining ½ cup flour; add to batter and blend well.

Spoon batter into 2 greased, flour-dusted 4½- by 8½-inch loaf pans or 4 greased, flour-dusted 3⅜- by 7⅜-inch loaf pans. Bake in a 275° oven until a wooden pick inserted in center of cake comes out clean (about 1½ hours; 1¼ hours for smaller cakes).

Let cool in pans on racks. If desired, spoon 2 tablespoons rum over each cake (1 tablespoon over each small cake) while cakes are still warm. To store, turn out of pans; wrap airtight and refrigerate or freeze. Makes 2 large or 4 smaller loaves.

Spiced Apple Fruitcake

Unlike most fruitcakes, this spicy version is made entirely with dried fruits—in particular, plenty of dried apples—rather than the usual candied cherries, pineapple, and peels. Applesauce makes the cake deliciously moist.

    1   package (8 oz.) mixed
        dried fruit, chopped
    1   package (6 oz.) dried
        apples, chopped
    ¼   cup brandy
    ½   cup water
    2¼ cups sugar
    ¾   cup *each* golden and
        dark raisins
    ¾   cup (⅜ lb.) butter or
        margarine, at room
        temperature
    3   large eggs
    1   teaspoon grated
        lemon peel
    1   jar (14 oz.) applesauce
    3   cups all-purpose flour
    ¼   teaspoon salt
    ¾   teaspoon *each* baking
        soda and ground cloves
    1½ teaspoons *each* baking
        powder and ground
        cinnamon
    1½ cups coarsely chopped
        walnuts, almonds,
        or hazelnuts
        Brandy (optional)

In a pan, combine mixed dried fruit, apples, the ¼ cup brandy, water, and ¼ cup of the sugar. Bring to a boil; then reduce heat, cover, and simmer until liquid is absorbed (about 10 minutes). Add raisins; set aside.

In large bowl of an electric mixer, beat butter and remaining 2 cups sugar until creamy. Add eggs, 1 at a time, beating well after each addition. Blend in lemon peel and applesauce. In another bowl, stir together 2½ cups of the flour, salt, baking soda, cloves, baking powder, and cinnamon; stir into creamed mixture. Combine dried fruit mixture, walnuts, and remaining ½ cup flour. Add to batter and stir to blend.

Spoon batter into 2 greased, flour-dusted (or paper-lined) 5- by 9-inch loaf pans or 4 greased, flour-dusted 3⅜- by 7⅜-inch loaf pans. Bake in a 325° oven until a wooden pick inserted in center of cakes comes out clean (about 1¾ hours for large loaves, 1 hour for small loaves).

Let cool in pans on racks. If desired, spoon 2 tablespoons brandy over each cake (1 tablespoon over each small cake) while cakes are still warm. To store, turn out of pans; wrap airtight and refrigerate or freeze. Makes 2 large or 4 small loaves.

Colorful Fruitcake Rounds
(Pictured at right)

Miniature home-baked fruitcakes make especially attractive gifts. These are baked in small juice cans; when they're sliced, big chunks of fruit and nuts show in a colorful pattern.

- 1 package (6 oz.) dried apricots, quartered
- 2 packages (8 oz. **each**) pitted dates, snipped into thirds
- 1 pound candied pineapple, cut into 1/2-inch pieces
- 1 package (8 oz.) **each** red and green candied cherries, halved
- 1 cup **each** walnut halves and whole almonds
- 1 cup Brazil nuts, cut into thirds
- 2 cups all-purpose flour
- 2 teaspoons baking powder
- 1/2 teaspoon salt
- 4 large eggs
- 1 cup sugar
- 1/2 teaspoon **each** vanilla and lemon extract

In a large bowl, combine apricots, dates, pineapple, cherries, and all nuts. Mix well; set aside. In another bowl, stir together flour, baking powder, and salt. Set aside. In large bowl of an electric mixer, beat eggs; gradually beat in sugar, vanilla, and lemon extract, beating until thick and lemon-colored. Beat in flour mixture until smooth (about 2 minutes). Pour batter over fruit and nuts, blending thoroughly to separate pieces of fruit.

Thoroughly grease 16 small (6-oz.) metal juice cans with a pastry brush. Pack fruitcake mixture into

*A **tempting selection of festive cakes** to bake for friends includes rich Eggnog Pound Cake and Cheesecake Petits Fours (facing page) and Colorful Fruitcake Rounds (this page).*

cans a few tablespoons at a time, filling all spaces; fill cans ¾ full. Arrange cans upright on baking sheets, 1 inch apart, and bake in a 300° oven until a wooden pick inserted in center of cake comes out clean (35 to 40 minutes). Let stand in cans on racks until cool enough to handle. Then remove bottoms of juice cans and gently push out cakes; let cool completely on racks. Wrap well and refrigerate for at least 1 week before slicing.

For individual rounds, cut fruit-

cakes crosswise into ½-inch slices with a serrated knife. For gift giving, heat-seal rounds in plastic wrap, if you like, following directions on page 14. Seal 12 individually wrapped rounds at a time, allowing 20 to 30 seconds per batch. Makes about 7½ dozen rounds.

Colorful Fruitcake Loaves

Prepare fruitcake mixture as directed for **Colorful Fruitcake Rounds**;

pack batter evenly into 2 greased 4- by 7-inch loaf pans. Bake in a 300° oven until a wooden pick inserted in center of cakes comes out clean (about 1 hour and 10 minutes). Let cool in pans on racks. Remove from pans, wrap well, and store for at least 1 week before slicing. Makes 2 loaves.

Cheesecake Petits Fours
(Pictured on facing page)

These dainty cheesecake squares are just two-bite size. Served plain or glazed with apricot jam and topped with sliced almonds, they make delicious pick-up-to-eat sweets for a tea or open house.

- 2¼ cups graham cracker crumbs
- ¾ cup sugar
- 5 tablespoons butter or margarine, melted
- 3 large packages (8 oz. **each**) cream cheese
- 1 tablespoon lemon juice
- 1½ teaspoons grated lemon peel
- 4 large eggs
- 1½ cups sour cream
- 1 cup apricot jam (optional)
- ½ cup sliced almonds (optional)

Combine graham cracker crumbs, 3 tablespoons of the sugar, and butter; mix well. Pat crumb mixture over the bottom of a rimmed 10- by 15-inch baking pan. Bake in a 350° oven for 5 minutes. Let cool on a rack.

In large bowl of an electric mixer, beat together cream cheese, remaining sugar, lemon juice, and lemon peel. Add eggs, 1 at a time, beating well after each addition. Blend in sour cream. Pour cheesecake mixture over crust and spread evenly.

Bake in a 350° oven until cheesecake looks set in center when pan is gently shaken (about 20 minutes). Let cool on a rack. Cover and refrigerate until cold (at least 3 hours) or for up to 2 days.

Using a sharp knife, cut into about 1½-inch squares. Draw knife smoothly across cheesecake; wipe blade after each cut. With a spatula, lift squares from pan onto a serving plate.

If you want to glaze the squares, heat jam in a 1-quart or smaller pan until melted, stirring. Spoon evenly onto top of each cheesecake petit four. Top each with 2 or 3 almond slices, if desired. Serve petits fours, or let stand for up to 2 hours; or refrigerate, uncovered, for up to 4 hours. Makes 5½ dozen; allow 3 or 4 pieces per person.

Eggnog Pound Cake
(Pictured on facing page)

Luscious-tasting pound cake is easy to make in a hurry when you start with cake mix and purchased eggnog. To enhance the festive eggnog flavor, we added a little extra nutmeg and rum.

- About 2 tablespoons butter or margarine, at room temperature
- ½ cup sliced almonds
- 1 package (about 18¼ oz.) yellow cake mix
- ⅛ teaspoon ground nutmeg
- 2 large eggs
- 1½ cups commercial eggnog
- ¼ cup (⅛ lb.) butter or margarine, melted
- 2 tablespoons rum or ¼ teaspoon rum flavoring

Generously butter a 10-inch fluted tube or Bundt pan, using about 2 tablespoons butter. Press almonds on sides and bottom of pan; set pan aside.

In large bowl of an electric mixer, combine cake mix, nutmeg, eggs, eggnog, the ¼ cup melted butter, and rum. Beat on medium speed until smooth and creamy—about 4 minutes.

Pour batter into prepared pan. Bake in a 350° oven until a wooden pick inserted in center comes out clean (45 to 55 minutes). Let cool in

pan on a rack for 10 minutes; then invert cake onto rack and let cool completely. Makes 10 to 12 servings.

Raisin-Nut Loaves

Baked in shiny foil pans, these moist, spicy little loaves are ready to give as gifts almost as soon as you take them from the oven. You might wrap the unfrosted cakes—pans and all—in plastic wrap, then decorate with bright ribbon bows. Or ice the loaves with Cream Cheese Frosting and present them, unwrapped, to favorite neighbors.

- 2 cups **each** sugar, water, and raisins
- ½ cup (¼ lb.) butter or margarine
- 3 cups all-purpose flour
- 1 teaspoon **each** baking soda, ground allspice, ground nutmeg, and ground cinnamon
- 1 tablespoon bourbon whiskey or water
- ½ cup chopped walnuts
- Cream Cheese Frosting (page 41), optional

In a 3-quart pan, combine sugar, water, raisins, and butter. Bring to a boil, stirring until butter is melted; then reduce heat, cover, and simmer for 10 minutes. Let cool to room temperature, but do not refrigerate.

Stir together flour, baking soda, allspice, nutmeg, and cinnamon; gradually add to cooled sugar mixture, mixing until well blended. Stir in bourbon and walnuts. Pour batter into 4 greased, flour-dusted small foil loaf pans, each about 3½ by 6 inches. Bake in a 350° oven until a wooden pick inserted in center of cake comes out clean (about 45 minutes). Let cool in pans on a rack. Spread with Cream Cheese Frosting, if desired. Or, to store, wrap unfrosted loaves tightly in plastic wrap and hold at room temperature for up to 2 weeks. Frost just before serving, if desired. Makes 4 loaves.

Pies & Tarts

Crisp autumn weather brings a harvest of winter squash, crunchy nuts, and even seasonal fruits like pears and persimmons. The holiday season is the perfect time to turn this bounty into wonderful pies and tarts. Choose from such traditional favorites as pumpkin pie for Thanksgiving and old-fashioned mincemeat pie for Christmas. Or try something a little different, like a cream-filled winter pear pie or a buttery tart featuring a mélange of golden brown nuts.

Old-fashioned Pumpkin Pie

Molasses lends rich, spicy flavor to this most traditional of pumpkin pies. For a delicious alternative with Southern flair, try our variation made with yams or sweet potatoes.

Flaky Pastry for a single-crust 10-inch pie (this page)

1   *can (1 lb.) pumpkin*
1¼ *cups half-and-half or evaporated milk*
2   *eggs*
⅓   *cup sour cream*
¾   *cup firmly packed brown sugar*
¼   *cup light molasses*
1   *tablespoon all-purpose flour*
1   *teaspoon ground cinnamon*
½   *teaspoon **each** ground nutmeg, ground ginger, salt, and vanilla*
¼   *teaspoon ground cloves*
1   *cup whipping cream*
¼   *cup chopped crystallized ginger*

On a lightly floured board, roll out Flaky Pastry into a ⅛-inch-thick round and fit into a 10-inch pie pan, making a fluted edge. To partially bake shell, cut a circle of foil to fit inside shell; place in shell and gently mold to fit. Fill with raw beans, rice, or pie weights. Bake in a 425° oven for 10 minutes. Lift off foil and beans and continue to bake until lightly browned (about 5 more minutes). Let cool on a rack.

In a large bowl, beat pumpkin, half-and-half, eggs, sour cream, sugar, molasses, flour, cinnamon, nutmeg, ground ginger, salt, vanilla, and cloves until smoothly blended. Pour into partially baked pastry shell.

Bake in lower third of a 425° oven for 15 minutes. Reduce oven temperature to 350° and continue to bake until filling is set in center when pan is gently shaken (40 to 45 more minutes). If crust browns too rapidly, cover edges loosely with foil. Let cool on a rack for at least 30 minutes. If made ahead, cover and refrigerate until next day; remove from refrigerator at least 30 minutes before serving.

Whip cream until it holds soft peaks; fold in crystallized ginger. Top each slice with a dollop of cream. Makes 8 to 10 servings.

Sweet Yam Pie

Follow directions for **Old-fashioned Pumpkin Pie,** but substitute 2 cups mashed **cooked yams** or sweet potatoes for pumpkin. Increase brown sugar to 1 cup; omit molasses. Omit crystallized ginger; garnish pie with **sweetened whipped cream** and sprinkle with chopped **cashews** or sliced almonds.

Flaky Pastry

This tender, flaky pastry will enhance many of your favorite pies. The recipe makes enough dough for a single-crust 9-inch pie; use the variation that follows for a double-crust 9-inch or a single-crust 10-inch pie.

1   *cup plus 2 tablespoons all-purpose flour*
¼   *teaspoon salt*
6   *tablespoons solid vegetable shortening or lard, or ¼ cup solid vegetable shortening plus 2 tablespoons butter*
3   *to 4 tablespoons cold water*

In a large bowl, stir together flour and salt. With a pastry blender or 2 knives, cut shortening into flour mixture until particles are about the size of small peas. (If using butter, cut into chunks; cut butter into flour mixture first and then add shortening.)

Pour 3 tablespoons of the water into a cup. Stirring flour mixture lightly and quickly with a fork, sprinkle water over mixture, a tablespoon at a time, stirring just until all flour is moistened. If mixture seems dry or crumbly, sprinkle with up to 1 more tablespoon water; dough should not be damp or sticky. Stir in a circular motion, scraping bowl bottom with fork, until dough clings together and almost cleans sides of bowl.

With your hands, gather dough into a ball. Flatten into a 4-inch round, wrap in plastic wrap, and refrigerate for 1 hour before rolling out. Makes one 9-inch single crust.

Double-crust Flaky Pastry

Follow directions for **Flaky Pastry,** but use 2¼ cups **all-purpose flour;** ½ teaspoon **salt;** ¾ cup **solid vegetable shortening** or lard, or ½ cup **solid vegetable shortening** plus ¼ cup (⅛ lb.) **butter;** and 6 to 8 tablespoons **cold water.** Divide mixed dough into 2 portions, one slightly larger than the other. Flatten each into a 4-inch round, wrap, and refrigerate as for Flaky Pastry. Makes one 9-inch double crust or one 10-inch single crust.

Harvest Moon Squash Pie

(Pictured on page 46)

Traditional in flavor and appearance, this pie looks like pumpkin but is actually made with winter squash. For smoothest texture and sweetest taste, use butternut, Delicata, Hubbard, Kabocha, or Sweet Dumpling. For a lighter gold color and mellower flavor, choose acorn, banana, Golden Acorn, or turban. As a special touch, top your pie with decorative pastry shapes or, if you like, fresh tangerine peel.

Butter Pastry (page 49)
2½ cups Baked Squash (directions follow)
¾ cup firmly packed brown sugar
½ cup whipping cream
3 large eggs
1 tablespoon grated tangerine peel
2 teaspoons finely chopped crystallized ginger
1 teaspoon vanilla
Finely shredded tangerine peel (optional)

Pinch off ¼ to ⅓ cup of the Butter Pastry dough and reserve for decorations. Press remaining dough evenly over bottom and up sides of a 9-inch pie pan, making a fluted edge. Set aside. To make decorations, pat reserved dough into a ball. On a lightly floured board, roll out dough into a ⅛-inch-thick round. Using a knife or cookie cutter, cut out decorative shapes. Place in a small pie pan and bake in a 350° oven until golden brown (about 15 minutes).

Meanwhile, whirl Baked Squash in a food processor or blender until very smoothly puréed. Add sugar, cream, eggs, grated tangerine peel, ginger, and vanilla; whirl until blended. Pour filling into pastry shell.

Bake on center rack of a 350° oven until filling is set in center when pan is gently shaken (50 to 60 minutes). If crust browns too rapidly, cover edges loosely with foil. Let cool on a rack for at least 30 minutes. If made ahead, cover and refrigerate for up to 2 days; remove from refrigerator at least 30 minutes before serving.

Garnish with pastry decorations or, if desired, shredded tangerine peel. Makes 8 or 9 servings.

Baked Squash. Cut **squash** (see below for varieties) in half; if shell is hard, tap knife with a mallet to drive it through squash.

Scoop out and discard seeds and strings. Cut large squash —banana or Hubbard—into 6- to 7-inch chunks. Lay squash halves or pieces, shell sides up, in a 10- by 15-inch rimmed baking pan. Bake in a 350° oven until pulp is tender and pierces easily (see below for baking time for each squash). Turn squash cut side up and let cool. When cool enough to handle, scoop pulp from shell and measure.

For each pie, use amount of squash given and bake for suggested period of time. Both measures are approximate.

Acorn: 2½ pounds; 45 minutes
Banana: 2 to 2½ pounds; 1 to 1½ hours
Butternut: 2 pounds; 1¼ hours
Delicata: 3 pounds; 30 minutes
Golden Acorn: 2¼ pounds; 45 minutes
Hubbard: 2½ to 3 pounds; 1½ hours
Kabocha: 2½ pounds; 50 minutes
Sweet Dumpling: 3 pounds; 35 minutes
Turban: 2½ pounds; 45 minutes

Traditional Mince Pie

Make a mince pie worthy of a Dickensian feast with real old-fashioned mincemeat, chock-full of beef, brandy, fruit, and pungent spices.

Flaky Pastry for a double-crust 9-inch pie (facing page)
1 quart mincemeat, homemade (recipe on page 46) or purchased

1 cup chopped walnuts
2 tablespoons brandy
Whipped Hard Sauce (recipe follows)

On a lightly floured board, roll out larger portion of Flaky Pastry into a ⅛-inch-thick round and fit into a 9-inch pie pan. Combine mincemeat, walnuts, and brandy; spoon into pastry shell. Roll out remaining pastry on a lightly floured board and fit over top of pie. Fold pastry edges together to seal; then flute. Cut several slashes in top.

Bake in lower third of a 425° oven until crust is golden brown (35 to 40 minutes). Let cool on a rack for about 1 hour; serve warm with Whipped Hard Sauce. Makes 6 to 8 servings.

Whipped Hard Sauce. In a bowl, blend together ¼ cup (⅛ lb.) **butter,** at room temperature; 1 cup **powdered sugar;** and 1 tablespoon **brandy.** In another bowl, whip ¼ cup **whipping cream** until it holds soft peaks; fold into creamed mixture. Cover and refrigerate for up to 12 hours.

Mincemeat Tarts

Homemade mincemeat tastes best in these tarts, but purchased mincemeat also works well—either the bottled ready-to-use type or the boxed condensed form, reconstituted according to package directions.

Flaky Pastry for a single-crust 9-inch pie (facing page)
1 small package (3 oz.) cream cheese, at room temperature
1 tablespoon sugar
1 tablespoon brandy or apple juice
½ teaspoon grated orange peel
1½ cups mincemeat, homemade (recipe on page 46) or purchased
⅓ cup chopped nuts

On a lightly floured board, roll out Flaky Pastry into a ⅛-inch-thick round. Cut into eight 4-inch circles (re-roll scraps and cut again, if necessary).

Drape pastry circles over bottoms of 2½-inch muffin cups (measured across top), alternating cups so pastry shells don't touch each other. Pleat pastry around cups; with a fork, prick bottom of each shell several times. Bake in a 450° oven until golden brown (7 to 8 minutes). Let cool completely before removing from pans.

In a bowl, beat cream cheese, sugar, brandy, and orange peel until smooth. Spoon an equal amount of the cheese mixture into each pastry shell. Stir together mincemeat and nuts; spoon about 3 tablespoons of the mincemeat mixture into each tart. Cover and refrigerate for at least 1 hour or until next day. Makes 8 small tarts.

Old-fashioned Mincemeat

If you plan to use this mincemeat in pies, freeze it in 1-quart containers. Pack it in smaller quantities for use in tarts.

1	pound lean beef stew meat, cut into 1-inch cubes
½	pound beef suet
2	pounds tart green apples (unpeeled), cored and quartered
¼	pound citron
1	orange (unpeeled), seeded
1	lemon (unpeeled), seeded

Topped with autumn leaves *cut from pastry and delicate curlicues of tangerine peel, these appealing Harvest Moon Squash Pies (page 45), made with your choice of winter squash, are the perfect ending to a Thanksgiving meal.*

1½	cups **each** granulated sugar and firmly packed brown sugar
1	package (15 oz.) **each** dark raisins and golden raisins
1	package (10 oz.) currants
½	cup dark molasses
2	cups **each** cider vinegar and apple juice

1	teaspoon **each** ground nutmeg, cloves, cinnamon, mace, and allspice
1½	teaspoons salt
2	cups brandy, or 2 cups apple juice and ½ teaspoon brandy flavoring

Place beef in a 5-quart pan and add just enough water to cover. Bring to a boil over high heat; reduce heat, cover, and simmer until meat is tender (about 1½ hours). Lift out meat and set aside. Measure cooking liquid; if necessary, boil to reduce to 1 cup (or add water to make 1 cup). Set aside.

Using a food processor or a food chopper fitted with a coarse blade, chop or grind meat, suet, apples, citron, orange, and lemon. Place in a 6- to 8-quart pan; add cooking liquid, granulated sugar, brown sugar, dark raisins, golden raisins, currants, molasses, vinegar, apple juice, spices, and salt. Simmer over medium heat, uncovered, until thick but still juicy (about 1¼ hours); stir often as mincemeat thickens. Stir in brandy; simmer, stirring often, until thickened again (about 30 more minutes). Remove from heat and let cool.

Spoon into freezer containers, allowing 1 inch head space. Cover and refrigerate for up to 1 week or freeze for up to 6 months. Makes 4 quarts.

Caramel-topped Apple Pie

Top this luscious pie with caramels purchased at a supermarket or try candy-shop or "gourmet" caramels, if you like. Either way, this apple pie is different *and* delicious.

Flaky Pastry for a
single-crust 9-inch pie
(page 44)
5½ cups peeled, sliced tart
    apples (about 2 lbs.)
¼   cup water
¾   cup **each** sugar and
    graham cracker crumbs
1   tablespoon all-purpose
    flour
½   teaspoon **each** ground
    cinnamon and nutmeg
½   cup chopped pecans
⅓   cup butter or
    margarine, melted
½   pound vanilla caramels
½   cup milk

On a lightly floured board, roll out Flaky Pastry into a ⅛-inch-thick round and fit into a 9-inch pie pan, making a fluted edge.

In a 3- to 4-quart pan, combine apples and water. Bring to a boil; boil for 1 minute and then pour into a 10- by 15-inch rimmed baking pan to cool quickly. Spoon apples into pastry shell.

In a large bowl, combine sugar, cracker crumbs, flour, cinnamon, nutmeg, pecans, and butter; sprinkle over apples. Bake in a 425° oven for 10 minutes. Reduce oven temperature to 350° and continue to bake until apples are tender when pierced (20 more minutes).

Meanwhile, combine caramels and milk in top of a double boiler. Stir over simmering water until melted and smooth. Pour caramel sauce over pie; continue to bake until caramel just begins to bubble at pie edges (about 10 more minutes). Let cool on a rack. Makes 8 or 9 servings.

Crisp Persimmon Pie

Bright orange, crisp-textured persimmons make a perfect pie to serve for Thanksgiving or Christmas dinner. Top with softly whipped cream for a delightfully different dessert.

8   cups peeled, sliced crisp
    tomato-shaped
    persimmons, such as
    Fuyu (about 2½ lbs.)
⅓   cup **each** granulated
    sugar and firmly packed
    brown sugar
2½ tablespoons quick-
    cooking tapioca
1   teaspoon ground
    cinnamon
½   teaspoon **each** grated
    orange peel and ground
    ginger
3   tablespoons lemon juice
    Flaky Pastry for a
    double-crust 9-inch pie
    (page 44)
2   tablespoons butter or
    margarine, cut into
    small pieces

In a large bowl, combine persimmons, granulated sugar, brown sugar, tapioca, cinnamon, orange peel, ginger, and lemon juice; stir to blend.

On a lightly floured board, roll out larger portion of Flaky Pastry into a ⅛-inch-thick round and fit into a 9-inch pie pan. Pour in fruit filling and dot with butter. Roll out remaining pastry on a lightly floured board and fit over top of pie. Fold pastry edges together to seal; then flute. Cut several slashes in top. Loosely wrap edge of pie with a strip of foil; set pie on a rimmed baking sheet.

Bake on lowest rack of a 425° oven for 35 minutes. Remove foil strip and continue to bake until juices bubble vigorously in center and pastry is well browned (about 20 more minutes). Let cool to room temperature before cutting. Makes 8 to 12 servings.

Cranberry Crunch Pie

This tasty holiday pie combines rich cream cheese, a sweet-tart cranberry-apple filling, and a spicy walnut streusel topping, all in one festive offering.

Flaky Pastry for a
single-crust 9-inch pie
(page 44)
1   large package (8 oz.)
    cream cheese, at room
    temperature
⅓   cup firmly packed brown
    sugar
2   tablespoons cornstarch
⅛   teaspoon salt
1   can (1 lb.) whole-berry
    cranberry sauce
2   cups peeled, chopped tart
    apples (about ¾ lb.)
    Walnut Streusel (recipe
    follows)

On a lightly floured board, roll out Flaky Pastry into a ⅛-inch-thick round and fit into a 9-inch pie pan, making a fluted edge. Prick shell all over with a fork, taking care not to pierce all the way through. Cut a circle of foil to fit inside shell; place in shell and gently mold to fit. Fill with raw beans, rice, or pie weights.

Bake in a 450° oven for 10 minutes. Lift off foil and beans and continue to bake until lightly browned (4 to 5 more minutes). Let cool on a rack.

In small bowl of an electric mixer, beat cream cheese until smooth; spread on bottom of pastry shell. In a bowl, combine sugar, cornstarch, and salt. Stir in cranberry sauce and apples. Spoon mixture evenly over cream cheese. Prepare Walnut Streusel; sprinkle over cranberry mixture.

Bake in a 375° oven until streusel is golden brown (about 45 minutes). Check pie after 15 to 20 minutes; if crust or streusel is browning too rapidly, drape pie loosely with foil. Let cool on a rack; then refrigerate until cold. Makes 6 to 8 servings.

Walnut Streusel. In a bowl, combine ⅓ cup **all-purpose flour,** ½ cup chopped **walnuts,** 3 tablespoons firmly packed **brown sugar,** and ¼ teaspoon **ground cinnamon.** With your fingers, rub in ¼ cup (⅛ lb.) firm **butter** or margarine until mixture resembles coarse crumbs.

Pear Pepper Pie

Winter pears, such as Bosc, d'Anjou, or Comice, lend a sweet, fresh taste to this rich, cream-filled pie. A light sprinkling of white pepper adds a mildly spicy accent.

Cream Cheese Pastry (recipe follows)

- ¾ *cup sugar*
- ¼ *cup quick-cooking tapioca*
- ¼ *teaspoon white pepper*
- 8 *cups peeled, thinly sliced firm-ripe pears, such as Bosc, d'Anjou, or Comice (about 3 lbs.)*
- 1 *egg, lightly beaten*
- ¼ *cup whipping cream*

On a lightly floured board, roll out larger portion of Cream Cheese Pastry into a ⅛-inch-thick round and fit into a 9-inch pie pan.

In a large bowl, stir together sugar, tapioca, and pepper. Add pears and stir gently; turn into pastry shell. Roll out remaining pastry on a lightly floured board and fit over top of pie. Fold pastry edges together to seal; then flute. Cut several slashes in top and brush with egg. Bake in a 400° oven until filling is bubbly (about 1 hour).

Cut a 3-inch-round hole in center of top crust and lift out cutout pastry; slowly pour in cream, lifting pears slightly with a knife so cream seeps in. Replace cutout pastry and let pie cool slightly on a rack. Makes 6 to 8 servings.

Cream Cheese Pastry. In a large bowl, combine 1 large package (8 oz.) **cream cheese,** at room temperature, and 1 cup (½ lb.) **butter** or margarine, at room temperature. Beat until smooth. Beat in ¼ teaspoon **salt.** Slowly stir in 2 cups **all-purpose flour** to make a stiff dough.

Divide dough into 2 portions, one slightly larger than the other. Flatten each into a 4-inch-wide round, wrap in plastic wrap, and refrigerate for at least 4 hours or until next day. Before rolling, let stand at room temperature just until pliable (dough should not actually reach room temperature).

Creamy Pumpkin Pie Squares
(Pictured on page 2)

When you're baking for a large holiday gathering, try this easy-to-make alternative to traditional pumpkin pie. You can make the crust a day ahead; then, a few hours before dinner, add the filling and the creamy topping, and bake.

- 1½ *cups all-purpose flour*
- ¾ *cup quick-cooking rolled oats*
- 1½ *cups firmly packed brown sugar*
- ¾ *cup (⅜ lb.) butter or margarine, cut into chunks*
- 3 *eggs*
- 1 *can (1 lb.) pumpkin*
- 1 *can (13 oz.) evaporated milk*
- 1 *teaspoon **each** ground cinnamon and vanilla*
- ½ *teaspoon **each** ground ginger, ground nutmeg, and salt*
- ¼ *teaspoon ground cloves*
    Sour Cream Topping (recipe follows)
- 1 *cup chopped walnuts or almonds*

In a large bowl, stir together flour, oats, and ¾ cup of the sugar. Using a pastry blender or 2 knives, cut butter into flour mixture until particles are about the size of small peas. Firmly press mixture over bottom and up sides, to within ¼ inch of rim, of a 10- by 15-inch rimmed baking pan. (At this point, you may cover with foil and let stand at room temperature until next day.)

Bake crust on lowest rack of a 350° oven until lightly browned (about 20 minutes). Meanwhile, in a bowl, lightly beat eggs. Add pumpkin, milk, cinnamon, vanilla, ginger, nutmeg, salt, cloves, and remaining ¾ cup sugar; stir until smooth.

Pour pumpkin mixture over crust, taking care not to pour any filling between crust and pan sides. Spread evenly with a spatula. Return to oven and continue to bake until filling jiggles only slightly in center when pan is gently shaken (about 20 more minutes).

Spread pie with Sour Cream Topping. Return to oven and bake for 10 more minutes. Sprinkle with nuts. Place on a rack and let cool to room temperature. If made ahead, cover loosely with foil and let stand for up to 4 hours. To serve, cut into squares. Makes about 15 servings.

Sour Cream Topping. In a bowl, stir together 1½ cups **sour cream,** 6 tablespoons **sugar,** and 2 teaspoons **vanilla** until smooth.

Nut Mosaic Tart
(Pictured at right)

What better way to showcase autumn's plentiful supply of nuts than in this spectacular golden tart? To enhance its rich, toasted flavor, top each slice with a generous dollop of sweet whipped cream.

    3   cups whole or half nuts
        (almonds, walnuts,
        hazelnuts, macadamias,
        pistachios, or pecans)
        Butter Pastry (recipe
        follows)
    3   large eggs
    1   cup honey
    ½   teaspoon grated
        orange peel
    1   teaspoon vanilla
    ¼   cup (⅛ lb.) butter or
        margarine, melted
        Whipped cream
        (optional)

Place nuts (if unroasted) in a 10- by 15-inch rimmed baking pan and bake in a 350° oven until lightly toasted beneath skins (break nuts open to check, if necessary), 8 to 15 minutes. Let cool. Prepare Butter Pastry and press evenly over bottom and up sides of an 11-inch tart pan with a removable bottom.

Rich and crunchy, *this showy golden tart boasts a harvest of toasted almonds, hazelnuts, and macadamias.*

In a bowl, combine eggs, honey, orange peel, vanilla, and butter; beat until well blended. Stir in toasted nuts. Pour into pastry shell. Bake on lowest rack of a 350° oven until top is golden brown all over (about 40 minutes). Let cool on a rack.

To serve, remove pan sides. Cut into wedges; offer whipped cream to top each serving, if desired. Makes 10 to 12 servings.

(If you shell your own nuts, count on getting about these amounts from 1 pound nuts in the shell: almonds—2 cups whole, halves, or chopped; walnuts—2 cups whole or halves, 1 to 1¾ cups chopped; hazelnuts—1⅓ to 1½ cups whole, halves, or chopped; macadamias—1 to 1¼ cups whole, halves, or chopped; pistachios—1¾ to 2 cups whole, halves, or chopped; pecans—2 to 2¼ cups whole or halves, 2 cups chopped.)

Butter Pastry. In a food processor or bowl, combine 1⅓ cups **all-purpose flour** and ¼ cup **sugar.** Add ½ cup (¼ lb.) **butter** or margarine, cut into small pieces; whirl (or rub with your fingers) until fine crumbs form. Add 1 large **egg yolk;** whirl (or mix with a fork) until dough holds together. Makes one 11-inch shell.

Candies

Visions of sugarplums belong to just about everybody's view of Christmas. And in these pages, we've gathered a collection of candies worth dreaming about: creamy fudge, tangy fruit bonbons, toffee topped with milk chocolate and hazelnuts. They're all perfect for holiday giving.

Creamy Vanilla Caramels

Creamy-rich, individually wrapped homemade caramels take time to prepare, but they're a marvelous gift for the candy lovers on your list.

- 2 cups sugar
- 1 cup light corn syrup
- 2 cups half-and-half or light cream, at room temperature
- ½ cup (¼ lb.) butter or margarine, at room temperature
- 1 teaspoon vanilla
- ½ teaspoon salt

In a heavy 3-quart pan, combine sugar, corn syrup, and 1 cup of the half-and-half. Bring to a full boil over medium heat, stirring constantly; then boil for 10 minutes, stirring.

Still stirring constantly, add remaining 1 cup half-and-half very slowly; mixture should continue to boil as you add half-and-half. Continue to boil for 5 more minutes, stirring constantly. Then add butter, about 1 tablespoon at a time, stirring; mixture should continue to boil.

Position a candy thermometer in caramel mixture; when temperature reaches 230°F, reduce heat to medium-low. Continue to cook and stir until temperature reaches 248°F. Immediately remove from heat and let cool for 10 minutes; then stir in vanilla and salt. Pour into a well-buttered 8-inch square baking pan. Let cool until firm.

With a knife, loosen candy around pan edges; then turn out of pan (if it doesn't come out easily, set pan over low heat for a few seconds). With a paper towel, wipe any extra butter off surface. Using a sharp, heavy knife and a sawing motion, cut candy into 1- by 2-inch pieces. Wrap individually in wax paper or plastic wrap. Makes 32 pieces (about 1½ pounds).

Chocolate Creme Fudge

A simplified method using marshmallow creme makes this creamy fudge just about foolproof. In very little time, you can make several batches for entertaining or gift giving.

For variety, you might want to change the basic fudge's flavor. We include easy directions for peppermint, chocolate-peanut, and butterscotch fudges—and even a "blond" fudge made with white candy coating and lightly accented with lemon peel.

We suggest cutting the fudge into squares for serving; you can also pat the squares into balls and roll them in finely chopped nuts or coconut.

- 1 can (5 oz.) evaporated milk
- 1⅓ cups sugar
- ¼ teaspoon salt
- ¼ cup (⅛ lb.) butter or margarine
- 1 package (6 oz.) semisweet chocolate chips
- ¾ cup or ½ jar (7-oz. size) marshmallow creme
- 1 teaspoon vanilla
- ½ cup chopped walnuts or pecans

In a 2½- to 3-quart pan, combine evaporated milk, sugar, salt, and butter. Bring to a rolling boil over medium-low heat, stirring; boil for 5 minutes, stirring constantly. (If heat is too high, mixture will scorch.)

Remove from heat; add chocolate chips and stir until melted. Quickly stir in marshmallow creme, vanilla, and walnuts until blended. Pour into a buttered 8-inch square or round baking pan; spread to make an even layer. Let cool, then cover and refrigerate. Cut into 1-inch squares to serve. If made ahead, wrap airtight and refrigerate for up to 2 weeks. Makes 2 pounds (about 5 dozen pieces).

Peppermint Creme Fudge

Follow directions for **Chocolate Creme Fudge**, but omit walnuts. Instead, stir in ⅔ cup crushed **hard peppermint candy**.

Choco-Peanut Creme Fudge

Follow directions for **Chocolate Creme Fudge**, but omit salt and butter; instead, combine 1 cup **crunchy peanut butter** with milk and sugar. Omit walnuts; add ¼ cup coarsely chopped **unsalted peanuts**.

Butterscotch Fudge

Follow directions for **Chocolate Creme Fudge**, but substitute 1 package (6 oz.) **butterscotch-flavored chips** for chocolate chips.

Blond Creme Fudge

Follow directions for **Chocolate Creme Fudge**, but omit chocolate chips. Instead, add 6 ounces **white candy coating** (for buying information, see Almond Bark, page 50), coarsely chopped, and ½ teaspoon grated **lemon peel**.

Peanut Butter–Brown Sugar Fudge

The world is full of peanut butter lovers—and any one of them would love a panful of this creamy fudge at holiday time.

    1   cup firmly packed brown
        sugar
    2   tablespoons butter or
        margarine
    1   cup granulated sugar
    ½   cup evaporated milk
    ¼   cup creamy peanut
        butter
    1   cup miniature
        marshmallows
    1   teaspoon vanilla
    ¼   cup chopped dry-roasted
        peanuts

In a 3- to 4-quart pan, combine brown sugar, butter, granulated sugar, and evaporated milk. Bring to a boil over high heat, then boil until syrup registers 234°F (soft ball stage) on a candy thermometer (about 5 minutes).

Add peanut butter and sprinkle in marshmallows; *do not stir.* Remove from heat and let cool to about 150°F. Add vanilla. With a wooden spoon, beat vigorously until mixture is creamy and loses its shiny appearance (about 5 minutes).

Quickly spread in a well-buttered 8- or 9-inch square pan. Sprinkle peanuts over top and press in lightly. Let stand, uncovered, until firm; cut into 1- to 1½-inch squares to serve. If made ahead, cover and refrigerate for up to 1 week. Makes 3 to 7 dozen pieces.

Hazelnut Chocolate Truffles

Think about making these enticing truffles for a friend who likes European-style milk chocolate—the kind that's flavored with hazelnuts. Made from hazelnut "butter" mixed with melted chocolate and egg yolks, they're very rich and very special.

(For the chocolate, you can use either bar chocolate or chips.)

    1   cup hazelnuts
    ¾   cup (⅜ lb.) butter or
         margarine, melted
    3   ounces **each** semisweet
         chocolate and milk
         chocolate
    5   large egg yolks
    1   cup unsifted powdered
         sugar
    1   teaspoon vanilla
         About 1 cup chocolate
         sprinkles or finely
         chopped nuts

Spread hazelnuts in a shallow baking pan and toast in a 350° oven until pale golden beneath skins (10 to 15 minutes), shaking pan occasionally. Let nuts cool slightly, then pour into a dishcloth and fold cloth to enclose. Rub briskly between your palms to remove as much of skins as possible. Chop nuts.

Pour 6 tablespoons of the butter into a blender or food processor. Add chopped nuts and whirl until very smooth and creamy, stopping motor periodically to stir nut mixture. Set mixture aside.

In a small pan, heat remaining 6 tablespoons butter until it bubbles and foams. Remove from heat, add semisweet and milk chocolates; stir until melted and smooth; set aside.

In large bowl of an electric mixer, beat egg yolks until foamy. Gradually add sugar, beating until mixture is thick; add vanilla. With mixer on medium speed, add nut-butter mixture, 1 tablespoon at a time, beating well after each addition. Then begin adding warm chocolate mixture, 1 teaspoon at a time, beating briskly after each addition. After 6 teaspoons have been added, increase additions to 1 tablespoon; when all chocolate has been added, continue to beat until mixture is well blended and smooth. Cover and refrigerate for 30 minutes.

Put chocolate sprinkles in a small bowl. Scoop out rounded teaspoonfuls of the truffle mixture and form into balls, then roll in sprinkles to coat. If made ahead, cover and refrigerate for up to 10 days or freeze for up to 1 month. Makes about 7 dozen truffles.

Apricot Slims

(Pictured on page 53)

Dried apricots, coconut, a spoonful of orange juice, and some chopped nuts are all you need to make these tangy delights.

    1   package (6 oz.) dried
         apricots
    ⅓   cup unsweetened grated
         or flaked coconut
    1   tablespoon orange juice
         About ¼ cup finely
         chopped almonds

If apricots are not moist, place them in a wire strainer and steam over simmering water for 5 minutes.

Put apricots through a food chopper fitted with a fine blade. Add coconut and put through food chopper again. Stir in orange juice and mix well. (Or combine apricots, coconut, and orange juice in a food processor and whirl until mixture begins to hold together in a ball—about 1 minute.) Divide mixture into 4 equal parts and wrap each in wax paper or plastic wrap. Refrigerate until cold and easy to handle.

To shape each part, sprinkle about 1 tablespoon almonds on a board; roll dough back and forth with your palms over nuts, forming a 16-inch rope. To serve, slice diagonally into 2-inch pieces. Makes 32 pieces.

Pear Slims

Follow directions for **Apricot Slims**, but substitute 6 ounces **moist-pack dried pears** for apricots; remove any bits of stem or core from pears. Instead of orange juice, use 1 tablespoon **lemon juice**; instead of almonds, roll each rope in about 1 tablespoon **unsweetened grated or flaked coconut**.

Fruit & Nut Slices
(Pictured on facing page)

A little less rich than many Christmas candies, these chewy treats will still satisfy a sweet tooth. To make them, you just grind together dried fruit, nuts, and coconut, then blend the mixture with peanut butter. (Use either creamy or crunchy peanut butter, as you prefer.)

8 ounces dried figs (about 1 cup lightly packed)
1 package (8 oz.) pitted dates
1 cup **each** raisins and unsweetened grated or flaked coconut
1½ cups chopped almonds or walnuts
1 teaspoon grated lemon peel
¼ cup lemon juice
1 cup peanut butter

Combine figs, dates, raisins, coconut, and 1 cup of the almonds. Put mixture twice through a food chopper fitted with a medium blade. Or combine ingredients in a bowl, then whirl in a food processor, a portion at a time, until mixture begins to hold together in a ball (about 1 minute); start and stop motor 4 or 5 times and push mixture down from sides of work bowl as necessary.

Add lemon peel, lemon juice, and peanut butter; mix well with a wooden spoon. Divide mixture in half and shape each half into a log about 12 inches long.

For each log, sprinkle ¼ cup of remaining almonds on a piece of wax paper and roll log in almonds to coat. Wrap tightly and refrigerate for at least 3 hours or until ready to serve; then cut into ⅜-inch slices. Makes about 5 dozen pieces.

Fruit & Granola Slices

Follow directions for **Fruit & Nut Slices**, but omit almonds. Instead, stir 1 cup **granola-style cereal** (break up any large lumps before measuring) into fruits after grinding. Coat each log with about ⅓ cup **granola-style cereal**.

Coconut-Date Logs
(Pictured on facing page)

Anybody who likes granola cereal will enjoy these goodies. Plenty of dates, granola, and nuts combine in crunchy little logs coated with coconut.

1 package (8 oz.) pitted dates, snipped
½ cup (¼ lb.) butter or margarine
1 teaspoon vanilla
¾ cup finely chopped walnuts, almonds, or pecans
¾ cup granola-style cereal (break up any large lumps before measuring)
About ⅔ cup unsweetened grated or flaked coconut

In a pan, combine dates, butter, and vanilla. Place over low heat and stir until butter is melted and blended with dates (about 4 minutes). Refrigerate just until mixture is firm enough to mold and shape. Mix in walnuts and granola.

Sprinkle coconut on a plate or a sheet of wax paper. To shape each candy, press about 1 tablespoon of the mixture into a log about 1½ inches long; then roll in coconut to cover completely. Makes about 3 dozen.

Walnut Nuggets
(Pictured on facing page)

A tray of tempting dried fruits—plump prunes, apricots, dates, and more—is traditional Christmas fare in many households. Here, those classic fruits are combined with candied cherries and lots of nuts in an appealing candy. For an extra-pretty finish, each piece is topped with a perfect walnut half.

10 ounces walnut halves or pieces
5½ ounces whole blanched or unblanched almonds
1 package (8 oz.) pitted dates
½ cup moist-pack pitted prunes
4 ounces (about ¾ cup) dried apricots
2 tablespoons lemon juice
5 ounces (about ¾ cup) red candied cherries, finely chopped

Pick out about 36 of the most perfect walnut halves or large pieces; set aside. Combine remaining walnuts and almonds; you should have 2½ to 3 cups. Then combine nuts with dates, prunes, and apricots. Put mixture twice through a food chopper fitted with a medium blade. Or combine ingredients in a bowl, then whirl in a food processor, a portion at a time, until mixture begins to hold together in a ball (about 1 minute); start and stop motor 4 or 5 times and push mixture down from sides of work bowl as necessary.

With a fork or your fingers, mix in lemon juice and cherries until well blended. Divide into 3 equal parts and roll each into a 12-inch log (refrigerate briefly if too soft to roll). Wrap each roll tightly in wax paper or plastic wrap and refrigerate for at least 3 hours or until ready to serve. Then cut into 1-inch sections, turn cut side down, and press a walnut half into top of each. Makes about 3 dozen pieces.

Make up a pretty trayful of sweets with refreshingly light fruit flavors this holiday season. From left to right on platter, here are Apricot Slims (page 51) and Walnut Nuggets, Coconut-Date Logs, and Fruit & Nut Slices (facing page).

Sugared Walnuts & Pecans

Sweet and crunchy sugared nuts are always a welcome treat. These are lightly spiced with cinnamon and nutmeg and sparked with a touch of orange peel.

- 4 cups walnut or pecan halves; or 2 cups of each
- 3/4 cup firmly packed brown sugar
- 1/3 cup evaporated milk
- 1/2 teaspoon **each** ground cinnamon and grated orange peel
- 1/4 teaspoon ground nutmeg

Spread nuts evenly in a large, shallow baking pan. Toast in a 350° oven for about 5 minutes; let cool.

In a pan, stir together sugar, evaporated milk, cinnamon, orange peel, and nutmeg. Bring to a boil over medium heat; boil for 2 minutes without stirring. Remove from heat; let cool for 3 to 5 minutes, then pour evenly over nuts in baking pan. Mix quickly until nuts are well coated. Spread nuts out again in pan and let dry for several hours; then lift with a spatula and break apart. Store airtight. Makes 4 cups.

Homemade Marzipan

As easily as you form dough into breads and rolls, you can turn lumps of marzipan into simple shapes— fruits, vegetables, conical trees, even piglets or chicks. The smooth nut paste, made from finely ground almonds, sugar, and egg whites, handles much like children's play-dough.

When you make your own marzipan from fresh almonds, it has a delicious natural nut flavor, remarkably different from the typical brightly colored, heavily flavored candy store confections. (It's less expensive than purchased marzipan, too.) Lightly browning the marzipan shapes in the oven brings out the flavor.

- 1 pound (about 3 cups) whole blanched almonds
- 3 cups sugar
- 3 large egg whites
- 1 teaspoon orange flower water
- 1/4 teaspoon almond extract
- 2 to 3 tablespoons light corn syrup
- 1 large egg yolk mixed with 1 tablespoon water

In a food processor or blender, whirl 1/3 of the almonds until powdery (there should not be any discernible pieces of nuts). Add 1 cup of the sugar and process until blended. Empty into a large bowl; repeat with remaining almonds and remaining 2 cups sugar.

Beat egg whites with a fork until frothy. Mix in orange flower water, almond extract, and 2 tablespoons of the corn syrup. Drizzle egg white mixture over almond mixture; mix thoroughly with a heavy-duty mixer on low speed or work mixture with your hands as if you were kneading dough.

Form marzipan into a ball; if it doesn't hold together easily, work in a little more corn syrup. Place in an airtight plastic container; refrigerate for at least 2 days or up to 2 weeks before shaping.

To shape marzipan, use about 1½ tablespoons for each piece, keeping in mind that very thick or very thin candies will not brown evenly. Place your creations on ungreased baking sheets. (At this point, you may cover lightly with plastic wrap and let stand at room temperature for up to 24 hours.)

To bake, brush *very lightly* with egg yolk mixture. Bake in a 400° oven just until bottoms are lightly browned (5 to 6 minutes). Then broil 3 to 4 inches below heat just until tops are browned to your liking; watch constantly so candies won't burn.

With a wide spatula, transfer marzipan to wire racks to cool. Serve; or package airtight and store for up to 1 week. Makes 2½ to 2¾ pounds (about 3¾ cups), enough for 40 to 48 pieces.

Almond Bark

Here's a confection that couldn't be much simpler to make: you just melt semisweet chocolate or white candy coating, then stir in whole toasted almonds.

White candy coating is sometimes called white chocolate; it's sold in most candy stores, at the candy counters of some department stores, and in some well-stocked supermarkets.

- 1 cup whole unblanched almonds
- 3 packages (6 oz. **each**) semisweet chocolate chips or 1 pound white candy coating
- 2 tablespoons solid vegetable shortening (do not substitute butter or other shortening)

Spread almonds in a baking pan and toast in a 350° oven for about 8 minutes, shaking pan occasionally. Let cool.

Line a rimmed 10- by 15-inch baking pan with wax paper, covering bottom and sides of pan.

Place chocolate chips or candy coating in the top of a double boiler. Add shortening; stir over barely simmering water just until mixture begins to melt. Remove from heat; stir until completely melted. Stir in toasted almonds.

Turn mixture into pan and spread to distribute nuts evenly; to spread more smoothly, drop pan onto counter several times from a height of about 8 inches. Refrigerate candy just until firm. Break into pieces before serving. To store, cover airtight and refrigerate for up to 3 weeks. Makes about 1¼ pounds.

Rocky Road

Like the popular ice cream, this quick-to-fix chocolate candy is studded with marshmallows and nuts. The recipe makes a lot, so you can give some away as gifts and still have a supply on hand for the family.

2 large packages (12 oz. **each**) semisweet chocolate chips or 24 ounces white candy coating

3 tablespoons solid vegetable shortening (do not substitute butter or other shortening)

1 bag (10½ oz.) miniature marshmallows

2 cups coarsely chopped nuts

Line two 8-inch square pans with wax paper, covering bottoms and sides of pans. (Or arrange 8 to 10 dozen paper bonbon cases on rimmed baking sheets.)

Place chocolate chips or candy coating in the top of a double boiler. Add shortening; stir over barely simmering water just until mixture begins to melt. Remove from heat; stir until completely melted. Stir in marshmallows and nuts.

Divide mixture between pans, spreading it evenly over pan bottoms; or drop by rounded teaspoonfuls into bonbon cases. Refrigerate just until firm. Before serving, cut candy in pans into 1-inch squares. To store, cover airtight and refrigerate for up to 3 weeks. Makes 8 to 10 dozen pieces.

Hazelnut-topped Toffee

Chocolate candy bars make a quick coating for this caramel-flavored toffee. You need to lay the chocolate atop the toffee as soon as it's poured into the pan—so have the bars unwrapped and ready to use before you start to cook.

1 cup (½ lb.) butter (do not substitute margarine)

1 cup firmly packed brown sugar

6 bars (1⅜ oz. **each**) milk chocolate

½ cup finely chopped hazelnuts

In a deep pan, combine butter and sugar. Cook over medium-high heat, stirring constantly, until mixture registers 300°F (hard crack stage) on a candy thermometer. Pour immediately into a buttered 9-inch square baking pan. Lay chocolate bars evenly over hot candy and let stand until softened, then spread into a smooth layer. Sprinkle with hazelnuts, pressing them in lightly with your fingers.

Refrigerate until chocolate is firm. Invert candy onto a flat surface and break apart into small pieces. Makes about 3 dozen pieces.

Chocolate Toffee

Bittersweet chocolate, plenty of pecans, and a full pint of cream go into a luscious candy that's sure to please even the sweetest sweet tooth.

3½ cups sugar

½ cup light corn syrup

½ cup (¼ lb.) butter or margarine

4 ounces bittersweet chocolate

2 cups whipping cream

1½ cups chopped pecans

1 teaspoon vanilla

Combine sugar, corn syrup, butter, chocolate, and cream in a heavy 3-quart pan. Bring to a boil; boil, stirring occasionally, until candy registers 290°F (soft crack stage) on a candy thermometer (about 1 hour). Meanwhile, sprinkle ¾ cup of the pecans over bottom of a buttered, shallow 11- by 15-inch baking pan or over a buttered marble slab.

Remove candy from heat and stir in vanilla. Pour immediately into prepared pan (or onto marble) and sprinkle remaining ¾ cup pecans evenly over top.

Let cool for about 10 minutes, then score in 1-inch squares with a sharp knife. Let cool in pan for several hours. Then invert pan and tap lightly to remove candy. Finish cutting. Set pieces in small paper cups or pack between layers of wax paper in an airtight container. Makes about 2 pounds.

Almond Toffee

Sliced almonds and almond extract flavor this rich toffee. Set each square in a little paper bonbon cup, if you like; or just arrange the candy in a pretty tin or other airtight container.

1 cup sliced almonds

2 cups sugar

¼ cup light corn syrup

1 cup (½ lb.) butter or margarine

½ cup whipping cream

1 teaspoon vanilla

½ teaspoon almond extract

Spread almonds in a shallow baking pan and toast in a 350° oven until nuts are golden (5 to 7 minutes). Set aside.

Combine sugar, corn syrup, butter, and cream in a heavy 3-quart pan. Bring to a boil, stirring. Reduce heat to low and simmer, stirring occasionally, until candy registers 290°F (soft crack stage) on a candy thermometer (about 1 hour). Remove from heat; stir in vanilla and almond extract. Pour into a well-buttered, shallow 9- by 13-inch baking pan or onto a buttered marble slab. Sprinkle almonds over top.

Let cool for about 10 minutes, then score in 1-inch squares with a sharp knife. Let cool in pan for several hours. Then invert pan and tap lightly to remove candy. Finish cutting. Set pieces in small paper cups or pack between layers of wax paper in an airtight container. Makes about 1 pound.

Festive Holiday Menus

∎

Good food and drink, high spirits and merriment abound during the holiday season. From the elegance of the Holiday Open House party (page 62) shown below to the cozy intimacy of a special Christmas Morning Breakfast, the menus and recipes in this chapter provide a wealth of ideas for all your holiday entertaining.

Easy Thanksgiving Banquet

(Pictured on page 58)

As autumn leaves scatter and the air turns chilly, the holiday season gets off to a delicious start with everybody's favorite meal—Thanksgiving dinner. In this easy-on-the-cook menu, your oven does almost all the work. You simply pop the turkey in to roast and then add, in sequence, onions, sweet potatoes or yams, chestnuts, and bell peppers. You can stuff the bird or not, as you like; pan juices make a simple gravy.

To start, choose a favorite green salad or offer one made with Belgian endive and watercress drizzled with a mustardy vinaigrette. For a spectacular finale, what could be better than our rich, old-fashioned pumpkin pie? This simple yet tasty menu will more than satisfy 8 to 10 hungry diners at your Thanksgiving table.

MENU
Endive & Watercress Salad
Roast Turkey with
All the Trimmings
Sherried Wild Rice Stuffing
(optional)
Cranberry Sauce
Crusty Rolls   Sweet Butter
Old-fashioned Pumpkin Pie
(page 44)
Chilled Dry White Riesling

Roast Turkey with All the Trimmings

1   turkey (12 to 14 lbs.), thawed if frozen
    Sherried Wild Rice Stuffing (optional; recipe follows)

2   or 3 **each** fresh rosemary, thyme, and oregano sprigs, **each** about 4 inches long, or 1 teaspoon **each** dry rosemary, dry thyme leaves, and dry oregano leaves

4   or 5 medium-size onions (unpeeled)

8   to 10 slender sweet potatoes or yams

2   cans (15½ oz. **each**) whole chestnuts in water, drained

4   or 5 large red or green bell peppers

½   cup (¼ lb.) butter or margarine
    Fresh rosemary clusters

Remove turkey neck and giblets; reserve for other uses. Rinse turkey inside and out and pat dry; then stuff with Sherried Wild Rice Stuffing, if desired, securing skin over opening and tying legs with string.

Place turkey, breast down, in a large (at least 11½ by 17 inches) shallow roasting pan (not on a rack). Place herb sprigs inside unstuffed turkey, on top of stuffed bird. Place pan on lowest oven rack. Roast, uncovered, in a 325° oven until a meat thermometer inserted in thickest part of thigh (not touching bone) registers 185°F or until meat near thighbone is no longer pink when slashed (3 to 3½ hours).

About 1½ hours before turkey is done, turn breast up. Place onions in pan around turkey. Pierce sweet potatoes in several places with a fork and place on oven rack above turkey. Bake until vegetables give readily when gently squeezed (about 1½ hours).

About 1 hour before turkey is done, scatter chestnuts in pan around turkey, pushing down into pan juices. Remove stems and seeds from bell peppers and tuck into pan around turkey. Bake until tender when pierced (about 1 hour).

With a slotted spoon, lift out onions, chestnuts, and bell peppers and keep warm along with potatoes. Lift turkey from pan, draining juices from unstuffed bird into pan. If turkey is stuffed, spoon stuffing into a serving bowl and keep warm. Place turkey on a large platter and let stand for 15 minutes before carving. Cut onions in half lengthwise. Slit tops of sweet potatoes and add a pat of butter to each. Arrange vegetables around turkey; garnish with rosemary clusters.

Skim and discard fat from pan juices; pour juices into a serving container. Carve turkey; pour juices over individual servings of meat and vegetables. Makes 8 to 10 servings.

Sherried Wild Rice Stuffing

2   cups wild rice

4   cups regular-strength hot turkey or chicken broth

1   tablespoon olive oil, or butter or margarine

8   slices bacon, diced

4   cups chopped celery

2   cups chopped onions

½   cup dry sherry

1   cup pecans, coarsely chopped or halved

Rinse rice with water and drain. In a 4- to 5-quart pan, bring rice, broth, and oil to a boil. Reduce heat, cover, and simmer, stirring occasionally, until rice is tender and liquid has been absorbed (about 50 minutes).

Meanwhile, in a wide frying pan, cook bacon over medium heat until crisp (about 5 minutes). Lift out, drain, and set aside; discard all but ¼ cup of the drippings. Add celery and onions to drippings in pan and cook, stirring often, until soft (about 10 minutes).

Add vegetables and bacon to rice and mix lightly. Stir in sherry; then mix in nuts. Let cool. Makes about 10 cups.

Here's a Thanksgiving feast *(page 57) that's simplicity itself to prepare. Succulent roast turkey is surrounded by baked onions, bell peppers, sweet potatoes, and chestnuts; fresh rosemary adds an aromatic garnish to the resplendent platter.*

Tree-cutters' Tailgate Picnic

When the weather is crackling-crisp and the yuletide season is drawing near, it's time for a trip to your local Christmas tree farm. To make the occasion extra festive and satisfy fresh-air appetites, put together this easy-traveling picnic lunch for your tree-cutting crew. The centerpiece is roasted chicken; you can buy it already cooked or roast it at home. Purple eggs and a bright corn-and-red-pepper salad add colorful and piquant accents; homemade biscuits round out a satisfying meal for four.

MENU
Roasted Chicken
Corn & Red Pepper Relish Salad
Pickled Beets & Purple Eggs
Poppy Seed–Herb Drop Biscuits
Butter
Carrot & Celery Sticks
Crisp Molasses Cookies
Milk or Sparkling Apple Juice

For the fastest start, pick up cooked chicken at the supermarket or a delicatessen; for four servings, you'll need two chickens, each about 1½ pounds (cut them in half to serve). If you want to cook your own chicken, buy a 3½- to 4-pound bird and roast it at 375°, allowing 20–25 minutes per pound, until a meat thermometer inserted in the thickest part of the thigh (not touching bone) registers 185°. When cool enough to handle, quarter the chicken for serving.

To make the meal, start the chicken if you are cooking your own, then start the eggs; they need to marinate for at least an hour, but will keep for up to 1 week.

While the biscuits bake, make the corn salad and cut up carrots and celery. Transport cold foods and beverage in one insulated chest; if the chicken and biscuits are hot, pack them in another chest. Buy thin crisp molasses cookies, or raid your supply of pre-Christmas baking.

Corn & Red Pepper Relish Salad

- ⅔ cup distilled white vinegar
- ¼ cup sugar
- ¼ teaspoon **each** celery seeds and mustard seeds
- ¼ cup minced onion
- 1 package (10 oz.) frozen corn kernels, thawed and drained
- ½ cup canned red peppers or canned pimentos, drained and thinly sliced
  Salt and pepper

In a 2- to 3-quart pan, bring vinegar, sugar, celery seeds, mustard seeds, and onion to a boil over high heat. Reduce heat to medium and simmer, uncovered, for 5 minutes. Remove from heat and stir in corn and red peppers; season to taste with salt and pepper. Let cool completely.

Serve, or cover and refrigerate for up to 1 week. Drain before serving, or lift from dish with a slotted spoon. Makes 2½ cups (4 servings).

Pickled Beets & Purple Eggs

- 1 can (1 lb.) whole pickled beets
- 4 hard-cooked large eggs, shelled

Pour beet liquid into a small deep bowl and add eggs, turning to coat well. Top with beets, cover, and refrigerate for at least 1 hour or up to 1 week. Turn eggs occasionally during first hour, then once every day or so to ensure a uniformly deep color.

To serve, lift eggs and beets from liquid with a slotted spoon. Makes 4 servings.

Poppy Seed–Herb Drop Biscuits

- 1½ cups all-purpose flour
- 1 tablespoon **each** baking powder and poppy seeds
- ½ teaspoon **each** salt and dry thyme leaves
- ⅓ cup butter or margarine, cut into chunks
- ¾ cup milk
  Butter or margarine

In a large bowl, stir together flour, baking powder, poppy seeds, salt, and thyme leaves. With a pastry blender, 2 knives, or your fingers, cut (or rub) in the ⅓ cup butter until mixture resembles coarse cornmeal. Pour in milk; stir until dough is evenly moistened.

Drop dough in ¼-cup portions about 1 inch apart in a greased 9-inch round baking pan. Bake in a 450° oven until tops of biscuits are well browned (15 to 18 minutes). Serve hot or cold, with butter. Makes 8 large biscuits (4 to 8 servings).

Tree-trimmers' Buffet Supper

Gather family and friends together to deck the halls and adorn your Christmas tree, then reward their artistic efforts with this elegant and festive buffet for eight. The handsome cheese-stuffed pork roast is made ahead, so the filling can cool until firm and easy to cut. You can also make the wild rice salad, mulled cranberries, and tempting raspberry tart a day or two before the party. Even the artichokes can be boiled or steamed in advance, leaving you free to join in the decorating from start to finish. (You'll need about 16 small artichokes—two for each guest.)

MENU

Pork Loin Stuffed with
Two Cheeses
Mulled Cranberries
Small Boiled or Steamed
Artichokes
Wild Rice Salad
French Bread
Raspberry Jam Tart
Gewürztraminer   Apple Juice

Pork Loin Stuffed with Two Cheeses

4   ounces cream cheese, at room temperature
4   ounces ripened or unripened goat cheese (such as Montrachet or Bûcheron)
1   teaspoon ground sage
½   teaspoon dry thyme leaves
1   boned pork loin end roast (about 3 lbs.)
12 to 15 large canned grape leaves, drained
    Thyme sprigs (optional)

In a bowl, thoroughly blend cream cheese, goat cheese, ½ teaspoon of the sage, and ¼ teaspoon of the thyme leaves; set aside.

Open roast and lay flat, fat side down. Cover with plastic wrap and pound with a flat mallet to make a 9- by 11-inch rectangle. Fill roast so you can reroll it to original shape. First, line meat down center with a double layer of grape leaves, extending leaves 3 to 4 inches beyond roast at each end. Then spoon cheese mixture down center of leaves and fold ends over filling, making sure there are no holes or thin pieces at roast ends where filling could seep out as meat cooks. Lap leaves over sides, forming a neat roll. Roll meat around filling to enclose closely but not tightly; tie.

Place roast, fat side up, in a 9- by 13-inch baking pan. Rub remaining ½ teaspoon sage and remaining ¼ teaspoon thyme leaves on roast. Insert a meat thermometer into thickest part of meat (not into filling). Roast, uncovered, in a 375° oven until thermometer registers 160°F (about 1¼ hours). Let cool; let stand until serving time (no longer than 4 hours). Serve at room temperature. (If you do not plan to serve meat within 4 hours, cover and refrigerate cooled meat; bring to room temperature before serving.) To serve, cut meat into ¾- to 1-inch-thick slices; garnish with thyme sprigs, if desired. Makes 8 servings.

Mulled Cranberries

In a 3-quart pan, combine 3 cups **fresh or frozen cranberries**, 1⅓ cups **sugar**, 6 tablespoons **orange-flavored liqueur**, and 2 **cinnamon sticks**, *each* about 2½ inches long. Cover and cook over low heat until berries are translucent (about 15 minutes), stirring gently until sugar is dissolved. If made ahead, cover and refrigerate for up to 2 days; serve cold or at room temperature. Makes 8 to 12 servings.

Wild Rice Salad

1½ cups wild rice
3   cups regular-strength chicken broth
⅓   cup salad oil
2   tablespoons raspberry or wine vinegar
2   tablespoons minced shallot or onion
2   teaspoons Dijon mustard
¼   teaspoon pepper

Rinse rice with water and drain. In a 2- to 3-quart pan, bring rice and broth to a boil. Reduce heat so liquid is just simmering; cover and cook, stirring occasionally, until rice is tender to bite and almost all liquid is absorbed (about 50 minutes). Let cool.

In a small bowl, mix oil, vinegar, shallot, mustard, and pepper. Stir into cooled rice. Serve, or hold at room temperature for up to 4 hours. If made ahead, cover and refrigerate for up to 2 days; bring to room temperature to serve. Makes 8 servings.

An elegant cheese-filled pork roast is the centerpiece for our festive Tree-trimmers' Buffet Supper. The roast, accompaniments, and dessert can be made ahead and will wait on your buffet table until the last bauble has been hung.

Raspberry Jam Tart

1 cup plus 2 tablespoons all-purpose flour

¼ cup sugar

⅓ cup firm butter or margarine, cut into chunks

1 large egg yolk

½ cup plus 1 tablespoon raspberry jam

⅓ cup (about 4 oz.) almond paste

3 large eggs, separated

¼ teaspoon baking powder

⅛ teaspoon almond extract

1 to 2 tablespoons sliced almonds

In a food processor or a bowl, combine 1 cup of the flour, 2 tablespoons of the sugar, and butter. Whirl (or rub with your fingers) until fine crumbs form. Add 1 egg yolk; whirl or stir with a fork until dough holds together, then press into a smooth ball.

Evenly press dough over bottom and sides of a 10- to 11-inch tart pan with a removable bottom. Bake in a 350° oven until crust is light gold (about 12 minutes). Spread ½ cup of the jam over bottom of crust.

In a bowl, beat almond paste, 3 egg yolks, remaining 2 tablespoons flour, remaining 2 tablespoons sugar, baking powder, and almond extract until smooth.

In another bowl, beat egg whites until they hold soft peaks. Beat about half the whites into almond batter, then fold in remaining whites. Pour batter over jam in crust. Spoon remaining 1 tablespoon jam onto center of mixture; scatter almonds over top of tart.

Bake in a 350° oven until tart is well browned (about 25 minutes). Let cool completely. If made ahead, cover and let stand overnight. To serve, remove pan sides; cut tart into wedges. Makes 8 servings.

Holiday Open House

(Pictured on page 56)

Christmas is the season to welcome good friends into your home for a warm and spirited get-together. Make this year's open house one to remember with a colorful, varied all-appetizer buffet for 24.

From plump Shrimp with Green Goddess Dip to savory little fila finger snacks, this menu offers something for everyone.

Our selection of crudités (for dipping along with the shrimp) features radishes, cherry tomatoes, snow peas, cucumbers, baby carrots, and red bell peppers, but you can serve any vegetable that's available and appealing. To serve Meat-wrapped Fruits, simply wrap peeled melon wedges in thin slices of prosciutto; wrap unpeeled apple and pear wedges, drizzled with lime juice, in thinly sliced mild coppa. (You'll need about ¼ pound of each meat for 1 melon and 2 apples or pears.)

As for beverages, you'll usually please everyone if you offer champagne, sparkling cider, club soda, and a selection of fruit juices and soft drinks.

MENU
Shrimp with Green Goddess Dip
Italian Eggplant Relish
Layered Cheese Torta
Thinly Sliced Baguettes
Basket of Crudités
Savory Fila Appetizer Pastries
Cheese-Mushroom Fingers
Meat-wrapped Fruits
Champagne   Sparkling Cider

Shrimp with Green Goddess Dip

2½ to 3 pounds cooked, shelled, deveined medium-size shrimp (30 to 36 per lb.)
    Green Goddess Dip (recipe follows)
    Whole chives

Arrange shrimp in a large bowl or on a platter; cover and refrigerate until serving time or for up to 4 hours. To serve, spoon Green Goddess Dip into a serving bowl and garnish with chives. Offer shrimp with dip. Makes 24 servings.

Green Goddess Dip. In a blender or food processor, combine 2 cloves **garlic**, minced or pressed; ½ cup *each* coarsely chopped **parsley**, **green onions** (including tops), and **watercress**; 1 teaspoon **onion salt**; 2 teaspoons *each* **dry tarragon** and **anchovy paste**; and 4 teaspoons **lemon juice**. Whirl until smooth. Stir in 1 cup *each* **mayonnaise** and **sour cream** until well combined. Makes about 3 cups.

Italian Eggplant Relish

1 large eggplant (about 1½ lbs.)
2 large red bell peppers
½ cup olive oil
1 large onion, finely chopped
1½ cups thinly sliced celery
3 cloves garlic, minced or pressed
¼ cup tomato paste
1 cup water
¼ cup red wine vinegar
1 tablespoon **each** sugar and drained capers
2 tablespoons coarsely chopped fresh basil or 1 teaspoon dry basil
1 cup sliced ripe olives
¼ cup pine nuts
    Butter lettuce leaves (optional)

Cut unpeeled eggplant into ½-inch cubes. Seed and dice bell peppers; set aside. Heat oil in a 12- to 14-inch frying pan over medium heat. Add eggplant; cover and cook, stirring occasionally, until eggplant begins to soften (about 5 minutes). Uncover and continue to cook, stirring often, until eggplant begins to brown (about 10 more minutes).

Mix in bell peppers, onion, celery, and garlic; cook, stirring often, until onion is soft (6 to 8 minutes). Add tomato paste, water, vinegar, sugar, capers, basil, and olives. Cook, stirring often, until mixture is very thick (about 10 more minutes). If made ahead, let cool, then cover and refrigerate for up to 1 week.

Pour pine nuts into a small frying pan. Cook over medium heat, stirring often, until lightly browned (about 5 minutes). Sprinkle over relish. Garnish relish with lettuce leaves, if desired; serve cold or at room temperature. Makes 6 cups.

Layered Cheese Torta
(Make 2 for the party)

2 large packages (8 oz. **each**) cream cheese, at room temperature
2 cups (1 lb.) unsalted butter, at room temperature
    Sun-dried Tomato Topping & Filling (recipe follows)

In large bowl of an electric mixer, beat cream cheese and butter until very smoothly blended; scrape mixture from bowl sides as needed.

Cut two 18-inch squares of cheesecloth; moisten with water, wring dry, and lay out flat, one on top of the other. Smoothly line a 5- to 6-cup straight-sided plain mold, such as a loaf pan, terrine, charlotte mold, or clean flowerpot, with the cheesecloth; drape excess over rim of mold.

Set two sun-dried tomato sections in mold bottom. With your fingers or a rubber spatula, make an even layer of ⅙ of the cheese mixture. Cover with ⅕ of the Sun-dried Tomato Filling, extending it evenly to sides of mold. Repeat until mold is filled, finishing with cheese.

Fold ends of cheesecloth over torta and press down lightly with your hands to compact. Refrigerate until torta feels firm when pressed (about 1 hour). Then invert onto a serving dish and gently pull off cloth (if allowed to stand, cloth will act as a wick and cause filling color to bleed onto cheese).

If made ahead, wrap airtight in plastic wrap and refrigerate for up to 5 days. Makes 14 to 16 servings.

Sun-dried Tomato Topping & Filling. Drain 1 jar (10½ oz.) **sun-dried tomatoes in olive oil**, reserving 2 tablespoons of the oil. Center 2 tomato sections in mold bottom for topping. Whirl remaining tomatoes with reserved oil in a blender or food processor until finely chopped.

Savory Fila Appetizer Pastries

1   *package (1-lb. size) fila (thawed if frozen)*
⅔   *cup (⅓ lb.) butter or margarine, melted*
     Spicy Lamb Filling (recipe follows)
     Feta Cheese Filling (recipe follows)

Unroll fila and lay flat; cut sheets in half crosswise and cover with plastic wrap to prevent drying.

Use half the fila for each filling. Work with a half sheet of fila at a time; lightly brush with butter before filling.

Fill and shape pastries as directed below, then place shaped pastries about 1½ inches apart on greased baking sheets. Brush tops with butter and cover with plastic wrap while shaping remaining pastries.

To shape lamb logs, fold buttered half-sheet of fila in half crosswise. Brush again with butter. Place 1½ tablespoons of the Spicy Lamb Filling along short end of each piece; fold in sides, then roll up dough jelly roll style.

To shape cheese triangles, cut buttered fila half-sheet lengthwise into thirds. Place 1 tablespoon of the Feta Cheese Filling in upper corner of each strip and fold corner down over filling to make a triangle. Fold triangle over onto itself. Then continue folding triangle from side to side all down length of strip, as if you were folding a flag.

(After shaping pastries, you may freeze them for up to 1 month. To freeze, place shaped pastries in freezer until firm; then carefully stack in a rigid container, placing foil between each layer of pastries. Do not thaw before baking.)

Bake pastries in a 375° oven until well browned and crisp (10 to 15 minutes; 20 to 35 minutes if frozen). Serve hot; or let cool to room temperature, then serve. Makes about 32 lamb logs, about 48 cheese triangles.

Spicy Lamb Filling. Place a wide frying pan over medium heat; crumble in 2½ pounds **lean ground lamb**. Add 2 large **onions** (chopped) and 4 cloves **garlic** (minced or pressed). Cook, stirring often, until onion is soft and meat is browned. Spoon off and discard any excess fat. Add ⅔ cup *each* **catsup** and chopped **parsley**; 1 cup **dry red wine**; 1 can (1 lb.) **stewed tomatoes**; and 1 teaspoon *each* **pepper** and **ground nutmeg**.

Cook, stirring occasionally, for 10 minutes. Increase heat to high and continue to cook, stirring constantly, until almost all liquid has evaporated. Remove pan from heat and let filling cool for about 10 minutes.

If made ahead, cover and refrigerate for up to 2 days; bring to room temperature before using.

Feta Cheese Filling. In large bowl of an electric mixer, combine 8 ounces **ricotta cheese**; 8 ounces **feta cheese**, crumbled (about 2 cups); 1 small package (3 oz.) **cream cheese** (at room temperature); 2 tablespoons **all-purpose flour**; 2 large

eggs; ½ teaspoon **ground nutmeg**; ¼ teaspoon **white pepper**; and ½ cup finely chopped **parsley**. Beat until mixture is well blended.

If made ahead, cover and refrigerate for up to 2 days; bring to room temperature before using.

Cheese-Mushroom Fingers

½   *cup (¼ lb.) butter or margarine*
1   *pound mushrooms, thinly sliced*
1   *large onion, finely chopped*
2   *cloves garlic, minced or pressed*
1   *large red bell pepper, seeded and chopped*
10   *large eggs*
2   *cups small curd cottage cheese*
4   *cups (1 lb.) shredded jack cheese*
½   *cup all-purpose flour*
1   *teaspoon baking powder*
¾   *teaspoon each ground nutmeg, dry basil, and salt*

Melt butter in a wide frying pan over medium-high heat. Add mushrooms, onion, and garlic and cook, stirring often, until onion and mushrooms are soft. Add bell pepper and cook, stirring, for 1 more minute.

In a large bowl, beat eggs lightly. Beat in cottage cheese, jack cheese, flour, baking powder, nutmeg, basil, and salt until blended; stir in mushroom mixture. Spread in a well-greased rimmed 10- by 15-inch baking pan. Bake in a 350° oven until firm (about 35 minutes).

Let cool for 15 minutes; cut into ¾- by 2-inch strips. Serve warm or at room temperature. If made ahead, cover and refrigerate for up to 2 days; reheat in a 350° oven until hot (about 15 minutes). Makes about 6 dozen.

Expandable Buffet Party

Is this the year you've decided to throw a really big holiday bash? If so, our expandable holiday buffet may be just the thing you need to make your party a roaring success.

Our basic menu serves 25 people but can be adjusted to accommodate multiples of that number; about 125 guests is the maximum. The chart below right shows how much food and drink you'll need for every 25 guests.

MENU

Cold Sliced Turkey, Ham,
Mortadella & Roast Beef

Cheese Tray

Mayonnaise, Mustard,
Whole Berry Cranberry Sauce

Three-Bean Salad
Marinated Mushrooms
Carrot & Raisin Salad
Fresh Fruit Salad
Pasta Salad

French Bread   Butter

Dry White & Red Jug Wines
Sparkling Water   Apple Cider

Double Cheese Bread
Pumpkin Bread
Spice Cake with Caramel Icing
Pork Sausage Cake
Seed Cake

Coffee   Tea

The party's simple framework allows you to do as much or as little cooking as you wish. We suggest you buy cold meats, cheeses, salads, loaves of French or other plain bread, and condiments to go with the assortment of delectable quick breads and cakes featured here. If you like to bake, you can make all our cakes and breads yourself; if you don't (or if you're short on time), you can purchase similar items from a bakery. Likewise, favorite homemade salads of your choice could certainly take the place of purchased salads.

Present a well-filled buffet table and plenty of small plates. Let guests help themselves, going back frequently to sample various combinations. Present the food in the following varieties and amounts.

Cold sliced meats. Fill trays generously with three or four kinds of meat and plan to replenish them for each 50 servings. Garnish with watercress, parsley, or lettuce leaves.

Cheeses. Choose three or four cheeses, such as Jarlsberg, Edam, Gouda, and jack. Serve cheeses whole or in large chunks. (Chunks of cheese stay fresh longer than slices or cubes.) As the party grows in size, buy bigger chunks rather than more variety. Place them all on the buffet at the beginning of the party, with knives for guests to cut the cheeses themselves.

Condiments. Limit the mustard selection to Dijon, which goes with everything. You can buy cranberry sauce or make it yourself.

Salads. Equal quantities of four or five kinds are appropriate. Choose a variety of purchased or homemade salads, all made with ingredients that won't wilt or darken on standing. Good choices include fresh fruit, pasta, potato, marinated vegetable, mixed bean, shredded carrot, cucumber, cabbage, and celery root salads. Plan to bring out refills for every 50 servings.

Butter. Soften sticks of butter, then pack into one or more crocks, smoothing tops so filled crocks look attractive.

Breads. Buy French bread or other local specialties, such as dark rye or whole wheat breads. Put out a complete selection and hold duplicates in reserve. Cut a few slices of each loaf to get guests started, then let them cut their own so breads stay fresher.

Desserts. Both of our sweet quick breads and all three fine-grained, boldly flavored cakes can be made weeks ahead, then stored in the freezer until party time. They take only about an hour to thaw. Decorate or ice the cakes shortly before serving; slice cakes and quick breads immediately before the party, keeping the slices together for an attractive presentation and to preserve freshness.

Quantities required for buffet supper party

Number of guests	25	50	75	100	125
Cold sliced cooked meats (pounds)	8	16	24	32	40
Chunks of cheese (pounds)	7	14	21	28	35
Mayonnaise, as a condiment (cups)	1½	3	4½	6	7½
Dijon mustard (cups)	½	1	1½	2	2½
Whole berry cranberry sauce (cups)	3	6	9	12	15
Salads (gallons)	3	6	9	12	15
Breads (5- by 9-inch loaves)	2–3	3–4	4–5	5–6	6–7
Butter (pounds)	½	1	1½	2	2½
Cakes (10- to 12-cup size or 9-inch-diameter two-layer cakes)	2–3	4–5	6–7	8–9	10–11
Wine (cases)	1	2	3	4	5
Mineral water (quarts or liters)	6	12	18	24	30
Coffee (cups ground; use 1 cup per 2½ quarts of water)	3½	7	10½	14	17½

Meats, cheeses, and salads galore *make an abundant buffet offering without a lot of fuss. Just pay a visit to your favorite deli or supermarket and select a pleasing combination of flavors, colors, and textures.*

Beverages. For convenience, have beverages at a separate self-serve station, along with cups, glasses, and spoons. Pre-chill bottles in large plastic garbage cans or bags filled with ice. To serve, place the bottles in ice-filled tubs. Borrow or rent electric coffee makers; remember that it takes 45 minutes to 1 hour for large machines to brew coffee. If you want to serve hot tea, have a coffee maker or large thermos filled with hot water and provide a selection of tea bags.

Double Cheese Bread

 ⅔   *cup (⅓ lb.) butter or margarine, at room temperature*

1⅓ *cups sugar*

 4   *large eggs*

 3   *cups all-purpose flour*

 1   *cup whole-wheat flour*

 4   *teaspoons baking powder*

 ½   *teaspoon baking soda*

 1   *teaspoon salt*

1½ *cups chopped walnuts*

 ⅔   *cup **each** milk and white wine (or use all milk)*

1½ *cups (6 oz.) shredded sharp Cheddar cheese*

 1   *cup (4 oz.) crumbled blue-veined cheese*

 1   *tablespoon **each** poppy seeds and sesame seeds*

In large bowl of an electric mixer, beat butter and sugar until fluffy. Add eggs, 1 at a time, beating well after each addition.

Stir together flours, baking powder, baking soda, salt, and walnuts. Add dry ingredients to butter mixture alternately with milk and wine. Divide batter in half; stir Cheddar cheese into 1 portion, blue cheese into other portion.

Grease and flour-dust two 5- by 9-inch loaf pans. Spoon half the Cheddar cheese batter into each pan, distributing down 1 long side; then spoon half the blue cheese batter alongside. Sprinkle poppy seeds over Cheddar cheese batter and sesame seeds over blue cheese batter.

Bake in a 350° oven until a wooden pick inserted in center of bread comes out clean (about 1 hour). Let loaves cool in pans for 10 minutes, then turn out onto racks to cool completely. If made ahead, wrap airtight and freeze; let thaw unwrapped.

To serve, carefully cut bread into ¾-inch-thick slices; it has a tendency to crumble. If you like, cut slices in half lengthwise. Makes 2 loaves (25 servings).

Note: If you prefer, you can make 1 Cheddar loaf and 1 blue cheese loaf; just put all the Cheddar batter in 1 pan, all the blue cheese batter in another pan. Bake as directed.

Pumpkin Bread

⅔ cup (⅓ lb.) *butter or margarine, at room temperature*

2½ cups *sugar*

1 can (1 lb.) *pumpkin*

3⅓ cups *all-purpose flour*

1 teaspoon **each** *baking powder, baking soda, and salt*

4 teaspoons *ground cinnamon*

2 teaspoons *ground allspice*

1 cup *raisins*

1 cup *broken walnuts or pecans*

In large bowl of an electric mixer, beat butter and sugar until fluffy. Blend in pumpkin.

Stir together flour, baking powder, baking soda, salt, cinnamon, and allspice. Thoroughly blend dry ingredients into pumpkin mixture, then stir in raisins and walnuts. Spoon batter evenly into a greased, flour-dusted 10-inch tube pan or 12-cup fluted tube pan.

Bake in a 350° oven just until bread begins to pull away from pan sides and a wooden pick inserted in bread comes out clean (about 55 minutes). Let bread cool in pan for 10 minutes, then turn out onto a rack to cool completely. If made ahead, wrap airtight and freeze; let thaw unwrapped. To serve, cut into about ½-inch-thick slices. Makes about 25 servings.

Everybody's favorite part of the buffet is the table of baked goodies. Here, the tempting offerings include (clockwise from top) Double Cheese Bread, Seed Cake, Pork Sausage Cake, and sliced Pumpkin Bread served with cranberry sauce.

Spice Cake with Caramel Icing

1   cup (½ lb.) butter or margarine, at room temperature
2¼ cups sugar
5   large eggs
3   cups all-purpose flour
1   tablespoon **each** ground cloves and ground cinnamon
1   teaspoon baking powder
½   teaspoon baking soda
1   cup sour cream
1   cup raisins
    Caramel Icing (recipe follows)
    Blanched almonds

In large bowl of an electric mixer, beat butter and sugar until fluffy; add eggs, 1 at a time, beating well after each addition. Sift together flour, cloves, cinnamon, baking powder, and baking soda.

Add flour mixture to butter mixture alternately with sour cream, blending in 2 or 3 additions. Stir in raisins.

Pour batter into a greased, flour-dusted 10-inch tube pan. Bake in a 350° oven just until cake begins to pull from pan sides and a wooden pick inserted in center comes out clean (about 1 hour). Let cool in pan for 10 minutes, then turn out of pan onto a rack to cool completely. If made ahead, wrap airtight and freeze; let thaw unwrapped.

Up to a day before serving, spread all the icing very thickly over top of cake; some will flow irregularly down sides. Decorate with almonds. To serve, cut into thin slices. Makes 12 to 16 servings.

Caramel Icing. Melt ½ cup (¼ lb.) **butter** or margarine in a 2- to 3-quart pan. Add 1 cup firmly packed **brown sugar** and ⅓ cup **half-and-half** or whipping cream. Quickly bring to a full boil; boil, stirring, for 1 minute. Remove from heat and let cool to lukewarm. Add 2 cups **powdered sugar** and beat until smooth.

Pork Sausage Cake

1   pound uncooked bulk pork sausage
1   cup raisins
1   cup chopped walnuts or pecans
1½   cups **each** granulated sugar and firmly packed brown sugar
2   large eggs
3   cups all-purpose flour
2   teaspoons pumpkin pie spice
1½   teaspoons ground ginger
1   teaspoon baking powder
1   cup water
2   teaspoons instant coffee granules or powder
1   teaspoon baking soda
     Pecan halves and candied cherries (optional)

In a large bowl, mix sausage, raisins, walnuts, sugars, and eggs. Mix flour, pumpkin pie spice, ginger, and baking powder. Stir together water, instant coffee, and baking soda. Add flour mixture and liquid alternately to sausage mixture. Pour into a greased, flour-dusted 10-inch tube pan or 12-cup fluted tube pan.

Bake in 350° oven until a wooden pick inserted in center comes out clean (about 1 hour and 25 minutes; lightly cover cake with foil if it begins to brown excessively). Let cool in pan for 10 minutes, then turn out onto a rack to cool completely. If made ahead, wrap airtight and freeze; let thaw unwrapped.

To serve, decorate with pecans and cherries, if desired. Cut into very thin slices. Makes 12 to 16 servings.

Seed Cake

¾   cup (⅜ lb.) butter or margarine, at room temperature
2   cups granulated sugar
4   large eggs
4   teaspoons grated lemon peel
3   cups all-purpose flour
2½   teaspoons baking powder
½   teaspoon ground nutmeg
1   cup milk
1   tablespoon **each** caraway seeds, poppy seeds, and anise seeds
     Powdered sugar

In large bowl of an electric mixer, beat butter and granulated sugar until fluffy. Add eggs, 1 at a time, beating well after each addition. Stir in lemon peel.

Stir together flour, baking powder, and nutmeg. Add dry ingredients to butter mixture alternately with milk; blend well.

Spoon about ¼ of the batter into a greased, flour-dusted 10-inch tube pan or 12-cup fluted-tube cake pan. Scatter caraway seeds on top. Cover with ⅓ of the remaining batter and sprinkle with poppy seeds. Top with half the remaining batter and sprinkle with anise seeds; spoon in remaining batter and smooth top.

Bake in a 350° oven until a wooden pick inserted in center comes out clean (about 1 hour). Let cool in pan for 10 minutes, then turn out onto a rack to cool completely. If made ahead, wrap airtight and freeze; let thaw unwrapped.

To serve, dust with powdered sugar and cut into thin slices. Makes 12 to 16 servings.

Easy-going Holiday Suppers

Casual good cheer reigns when you put on one of these easy-going holiday finger feasts for your friends or family. One supper features fresh cracked crab and artichokes to dunk in melted butter; the other is a hearty beef rib feast that ends with a rich, spicy, zabaglione-topped pudding. Both meals are easy on the cook; many of the foods can be prepared ahead or even purchased already cooked.

So all guests can reach the food easily, seat no more than six per table; duplicate the setup for more people. To get everybody into the spirit, hand out large napkins or bibs and provide finger bowls with small damp towels.

MENU #1

Cracked Crab with
Melted Butter
Cooked Artichoke Halves
French or Sourdough Bread
Butter
Sauvignon Blanc or
Pinot Chardonnay
Mincemeat Tarts
Rum Eggnog

Buy the crab cracked, cook the artichokes the day before, and buy the tarts and eggnog. Instead of crab, you could serve large boiled shrimp in the shell.

Cracked Crab with Melted Butter

Allow about 1½ pounds (or 1 small) **cooked Dungeness crab** in the shell for each serving. Have crabs cleaned and cracked at the market.

At home, rinse crab under cool running water to remove loose bits of shell. Pile crab into a wide serving bowl; if desired, rinse crab backs and lay on top as garnish. Serve, or cover and refrigerate for up to 6 hours.

Melt about ⅓ cup **butter** or margarine for each serving. As you shell crab to eat, dip meat into warm melted butter.

Cooked Artichoke Halves

Select 4 to 6 very large **artichokes**. Break off small outer leaves (bracts), then cut off thorny tips of artichokes with a knife. Use scissors to snip thorns from remaining outer leaves. Peel stem and trim off the end. Cut each artichoke in half lengthwise and cut out the fuzzy "choke." At once, drop artichokes in acid water to cover (2 tablespoons **vinegar** for each 4 cups **water**).

When all artichokes are trimmed, place them in a 5- to 6-quart pan. Add 8 cups **water**, 3 tablespoons **olive oil**, 2 tablespoons **vinegar**, ½ teaspoon *each* **dry thyme leaves** and **dry rosemary**, 1 teaspoon **mustard seeds**, 2 **bay leaves**, ½ teaspoon **whole black peppercorns**, 8 **whole allspice**, and 6 **whole cloves**. Cover and bring to a boil, then reduce heat and simmer until artichoke bottoms are just tender when pierced (30 to 40 minutes).

Lift from water; serve hot or at room temperature. Or let cool, then cover and refrigerate; bring to room temperature to serve. To eat, dip leaves and bottom into the melted butter served with the crab. Makes 4 to 6 servings.

MENU #2

Roast Ribs
Roasted Potato Balls
Edible-pod Peas
Black Bread   Butter
Cabernet Sauvignon or Barbera
Steamed Pudding with
Zabaglione Sauce
Brandy   Nuts in Shells

Cutting the potatoes is the most time-consuming chore, but you can do it the day before. Make the steamed pudding at least a day ahead, or buy it.

Because the beef ribs tend to smoke when cooking, be sure your kitchen venting system is working.

For a showy presentation, whip up the zabaglione at the table over an alcohol flame, then pour it over the warm pudding.

Roast Ribs

Have your butcher prepare 9 to 10 pounds **beef ribs** in large sections (6 to 7 ribs per piece). Mix together 2 teaspoons *each* **dry rosemary**, **dry thyme leaves**, and **rubbed sage**. Rub herbs over all surfaces of ribs. Sprinkle lightly with **salt** and **pepper**.

Arrange ribs in a single layer on racks in roasting pans (you need 2 pans, each at least 12 by 15 inches); ribs may have to overlap slightly. Roast in a 500° oven until meat between ribs is done to your liking (cut to test); allow 25 minutes for rare, 35 minutes for well done. Fat from meat smokes as ribs cook, so have venting system on high. Cut between ribs to serve. Makes 6 servings.

Roasted Potato Balls

Peel 12 pounds large **thin-skinned potatoes**. Cut into ¾- to 1-inch balls with a melon baller, or cut into ¾- to 1-inch cubes with a knife; save scraps for soup or to pan-fry. To prevent darkening, immerse potatoes in water as you cut them. (At this point, you may cover and refrigerate until next day.)

Pour ¾ cup (⅜ lb.) melted **butter** or extra-virgin olive oil into 2 rimmed 10- by 15-inch baking pans. Drain potatoes, add to pans, and stir to coat with fat. To each pan, add a 6- to 8-inch sprig of **fresh rosemary** or 1 teaspoon dry rosemary. Bake in a 500° oven until potatoes are golden brown and tender when pierced (about 1 hour). Shake pans occasionally to turn potatoes, or turn them gently with a wide spatula (stirring breaks off the brown surface). If made ahead, keep warm for up to 45 minutes. Turn into warmed serving dishes and season to taste with **salt**. Makes 6 servings.

Edible-pod Peas

Remove ends and strings from 1½ pounds **edible-pod peas** (use Chinese pea pods, also called snow or sugar peas; or use sugar-snap peas). Rinse peas. Bring to a boil enough **water** to cover peas; add peas to water and cook, uncovered, just until bright green and tender-crisp to bite (1 to 2 minutes). Drain at once and immerse in **cold water**, mixing gently to cool peas. Drain and serve. If made ahead, cover and refrigerate until next day. Makes 6 servings.

Steamed Pudding with Zabaglione Sauce

Prepare **steamed pudding** for 6 from your favorite recipe or from the Persimmon Pudding recipe on page 87, or purchase it. Heat to serve.

To make the sauce, put 4 large **egg yolks**, ¼ cup **dry white wine**, 3 tablespoons **sugar**, and 1 tablespoon **brandy** in a round-bottomed pan (or a metal bowl that can be set over direct heat—hold it steady with a potholder). Using a wire whisk, beat ingredients over direct heat (medium on a stove or an alcohol flame) until sauce is about tripled in volume and holds an impression when whisk is lifted (3 to 4 minutes). Pour warm sauce over pudding. Makes 6 servings.

A high-spirited evening's in store when you put together an easy-on-the-cook feast like this one, which features fresh cracked crab and artichokes to dunk in butter.

Holiday Potluck Supper

■

One easy way to gather friends together for a dinner party is to stage a potluck. Our menu provides a hearty and balanced supper for 12 to 15. As the host or hostess, you make the main course—a roast turkey with savory stuffing. Ask each guest to select one of the accompaniments; you supply the recipe. For the salad, simply ask someone to bring mixed greens with a favorite vinaigrette dressing. All dishes are easy to make ahead and transport, and all can be completed or reheated at your house with very little fuss.

MENU

Shrimp Cheese Stack
Turkey with Stuffing
on the Outside
Brown Giblet Gravy
Mashed Potato Casserole
Savory Green Beans & Tomatoes
Mixed Greens with Vinaigrette
Spicy Frozen Pumpkin Squares
Chilled Dry White Wine
Coffee

Shrimp Cheese Stack

2 large packages (8 oz.
   each) cream cheese, at
   room temperature
2 tablespoons
   Worcestershire
¼ teaspoon grated
   lemon peel
1 tablespoon lemon juice
½ cup thinly sliced green
   onions (including tops)
⅛ teaspoon liquid hot
   pepper seasoning
1 bottle (12 oz.) tomato-
   based chili sauce
1 tablespoon prepared
   horseradish
¾ pound small cooked
   shrimp
   Assorted crackers

In a bowl, beat cream cheese, Worcestershire, lemon peel, lemon juice, onions, and hot pepper seasoning until smooth. Spread on a 10- to 12-inch rimmed serving plate. (At this point, you may cover and refrigerate until next day.)

Just before serving, stir together chili sauce and horseradish; spread over cheese layer. Top with shrimp and serve with crackers. Makes 12 to 15 servings.

Turkey with Stuffing on the Outside

1 turkey (14 to 24 lbs.),
   thawed if frozen
   Salt and pepper
   About ¼ cup (⅛ lb.)
   butter or margarine,
   at room temperature
   Homemade Bread
   Stuffing (recipe follows)
   Brown Giblet Gravy
   (recipe follows)

Remove turkey neck and giblets; reserve for gravy. Rinse turkey inside and out; pat dry. Sprinkle cavities of bird with salt and pepper. Place untrussed bird, breast down, on a V-shaped rack in a roasting pan (at least 11 by 15 inches). Skewer neck skin against back. Rub all over with some of the butter.

Roast in a 325° oven, uncovered; allow 15 minutes per pound for turkeys weighing up to 16 pounds, 12 minutes per pound for birds 16 pounds and over. Baste turkey several times with butter during roasting. When bird is done, a meat thermometer inserted in thickest part of thigh (not touching bone) should register 185°F; internal temperature of breast should be 165°F.

About 1½ hours before turkey is due to be done, remove from oven. Tilt rack, draining all juices from bird, then lift bird and rack to another pan. Scrape all drippings from roasting pan and reserve.

Lift turkey from rack and place, breast up, directly in roasting pan. Rub breast with more butter. Return to oven; meanwhile, prepare broth for Brown Giblet Gravy (recipe follows). Continue to roast turkey; spoon Homemade Bread Stuffing around bird 45 minutes to 1 hour before it's done (when turkey is done, stuffing should be heated through and crusty on top).

Skim and discard all fat from reserved pan juices and use juices in Brown Giblet Gravy. Before carving, let turkey and stuffing stand for about 20 minutes, draped with foil. (It can stand longer if necessary.) To serve, lift turkey to a large platter and place stuffing alongside. Serve with hot gravy. Makes 12 to 15 servings.

Homemade Bread Stuffing. Melt ¼ cup (⅛ lb.) **butter** or margarine in a wide frying pan over medium heat. Add 3 large **onions**, chopped; cook, stirring, until soft. Then add ½ cup (¼ lb.) **butter** or margarine, 1½ teaspoons **dry marjoram leaves**, and ¾ teaspoon *each* **dry rubbed sage**, **dry thyme leaves**, and **pepper**. Set aside.

In a 5-quart container, combine 3 quarts day-old **whole wheat or white bread cubes**, 2 cups chopped **celery**, and ½ cup chopped **parsley**. Add onion mixture; toss to coat bread. Season with **salt**. Makes about 3 quarts.

Brown Giblet Gravy. Melt ¼ cup (⅛ lb.) **butter** or margarine in a 3-quart pan; add **turkey liver** and cook, turning as needed, just until firm. Remove from pan and chop.

Thinly slice **turkey heart and gizzard**; add to pan along with 2 **carrots**, finely chopped; 1 **onion**, finely chopped; and ½ cup finely chopped **parsley**. Cook over high heat, stirring, until mixture is very well browned. Pour in ¼ cup **dry sherry** or dry vermouth; boil until liquid has evaporated.

Add **turkey neck** and 6 cups **regular-strength chicken broth**. Bring to a boil; then reduce heat, cover, and simmer for 1½ hours.

Pour broth mixture through a wire strainer set over a bowl; discard residue and return liquid to pan. Pour in reserved **juices from roast turkey** (skimmed of fat). Bring to a full boil. Meanwhile, stir together 4 to 6 tablespoons **cornstarch** and 6 tablespoons **water**. When broth mixture comes to a boil, stir in as much of the cornstarch mixture as needed to make a medium-thick gravy. When gravy is thickened, stir in chopped turkey liver. Makes about 6 cups.

Mashed Potato Casserole

4½ to 5 pounds russet potatoes (about 8 large potatoes)
1 large package (8 oz.) cream cheese, at room temperature
1 cup sour cream
2 teaspoons garlic salt
½ teaspoon pepper
¼ cup (⅛ lb.) butter or margarine
   Paprika

Peel potatoes. In a 5-quart pan, bring about 2 inches water to a boil; add potatoes, cover, and boil until tender throughout when pierced (about 40 minutes). Drain, then mash well.

In small bowl of an electric mixer, beat cream cheese and sour cream until smooth; gradually add to potatoes, beating until smoothly blended. Beat in garlic salt and pepper. Turn mixture into a buttered shallow 3- to 4-quart casserole. Dot with ¼ cup butter; sprinkle lightly with paprika. Cover with lid or foil. (At this point, you may refrigerate for up to 3 days; bring to room temperature before baking.)

Bake, covered, in a 400° oven until heated through (50 to 60 minutes). Makes 12 to 15 servings.

Savory Green Beans & Tomatoes

2½ pounds green or wax beans, cut into 2-inch pieces
4 large tomatoes
10 tablespoons (¼ lb. plus 2 tablespoons) butter or margarine
1 large onion, chopped
½ pound mushrooms, sliced
3 cloves garlic, minced or pressed
1 teaspoon salt
1½ teaspoons **each** dry basil and dry oregano leaves
1½ cups soft bread crumbs
⅓ cup grated Parmesan cheese

Arrange beans on a steaming rack over 1 inch of boiling water; cover and steam until tender when pierced (8 to 10 minutes). Rinse in cold water, drain, and set aside. Cut tomatoes into thin wedges; set aside.

Melt ¼ cup of the butter in a wide frying pan over medium-high heat. Add onion, mushrooms, and ⅔ of the garlic. Cook, stirring, until onion is soft and all liquid has evaporated. Stir in salt and 1 teaspoon *each* of the basil and oregano. Combine mushroom mixture with beans and tomatoes; transfer to a shallow 3-quart baking dish.

Melt remaining 6 tablespoons butter in a small pan. Stir in remaining garlic, bread crumbs, cheese, and remaining ½ teaspoon basil and oregano. Cover with lid or foil. (At this point, you may refrigerate beans and topping separately for up to 2 days.)

Sprinkle crumb mixture over beans. Bake, covered, in a 400° oven for 20 minutes (30 minutes if refrigerated); uncover and bake until heated through (about 5 more minutes). Makes 12 to 15 servings.

Spicy Frozen Pumpkin Squares

2½ cups gingersnap cookie crumbs (about 45 2¼-inch cookies)
½ cup (¼ lb.) butter or margarine, melted
2 quarts vanilla ice cream, softened
1 can (1 lb.) pumpkin
⅔ cup firmly packed brown sugar
½ teaspoon salt
1 teaspoon **each** ground cinnamon, ginger, and cloves
½ cup chopped nuts

In a 9- by 13-inch baking pan, stir together cookie crumbs and butter. Press evenly over bottom and 1 inch up sides.

In a 4- to 5-quart bowl, combine ice cream, pumpkin, sugar, salt, cinnamon, ginger, and cloves; beat until well blended. Pour mixture into crust; sprinkle with nuts. Cover tightly with foil and freeze for at least 8 hours or up to 1 week. To serve, let stand at room temperature for 20 minutes; then cut into squares. Makes 12 to 15 servings.

Children's Christmas Party

A friendly caterpillar, a drift of fluffy white snowflakes, and sugarplum visions are the imaginative elements in this lively Christmas party for 10 children. The sinuous caterpillar sandwich contains your choice of two simple fillings; both can be made a day ahead. Bite-size balls of rich hazelnut or almond paste dipped in dark chocolate make the sugarplums; the hot milk drink is spiced with cinnamon and orange peel (offer a fruit punch, too, if you like). Make popcorn to fill the role of snowflakes; purchase cellophane-wrapped candy canes. Alongside the sweets, offer a basket of your young guests' favorite fruits—perhaps bananas, apples, pears, and easy-to-peel tangerines.

MENU
*Caterpillar Sandwich with Ham
or Tuna Filling
Chocolate-dipped Sugarplums
Popcorn Snowflakes
Candy Canes
Spiced Milk   Fruit Punch
Fruit Basket*

Caterpillar Sandwich

10   small soft dinner rolls, **each** about 3 inches in diameter

     Ham Salad or Tuna-Carrot Salad (recipes follow)

21   pitted ripe olives or seedless grapes

 2   small celery sticks

Split each roll in half horizontally; fill rolls with your choice of ham or tuna salad. Arrange filled rolls in an "S" shape on a serving tray. Spear olives on wooden picks; push 2 olives into either side of each roll for legs (or simply set olives alongside rolls). Push remaining olive, cut in halves, into front roll for eyes. For antennae, push celery sticks into front roll. You may assemble the sandwich up to 1 hour ahead, then cover it with a damp cloth and hold at room temperature until serving time. Makes 10 servings.

Ham Salad. In a bowl, blend 2 cups **ground cooked ham**, ½ cup **mayonnaise**, ⅓ cup **sweet pickle relish**, and 1 teaspoon *each* **prepared mustard** and **Worcestershire**. If made ahead, cover and refrigerate until next day. Makes 2 cups.

Tuna-Carrot Salad. In a bowl, combine 1 can (9¼ oz.) **solid-pack tuna**, drained and flaked; ½ cup *each* chopped **sweet pickles** and **mayonnaise**; and ¾ cup coarsely shredded peeled **carrot**. Stir gently to blend. If made ahead, cover and refrigerate until next day. Makes 2 cups.

Chocolate-dipped Sugarplums

1   pound (3½ cups) hazelnuts, whole or in large pieces; or 3 cups whole blanched almonds

2   cups powdered sugar

5   to 6 tablespoons egg whites (whites of about 3 large eggs)

     About 6 ounces semisweet chocolate chips

Spread hazelnuts in a shallow baking pan. Toast in a 350° oven until pale golden beneath skins (10 to 15 minutes), shaking pan occasionally. (If using almonds, toast for 8 to 10 minutes.) Let nuts cool slightly, then pour into a dishcloth and fold cloth to enclose. Rub briskly to remove as much of skins as possible (omit this step if using almonds). Lift nuts from cloth and let cool.

Coarsely chop nuts. Then, in a food processor or blender, grind nuts, about ⅓ at a time, until mealy.

Return all nuts to food processor and add sugar and 5 tablespoons egg whites. Process until a paste forms, adding more egg whites as needed. (Or mix ground nuts with egg whites and sugar with a heavy-duty mixer on low speed; or knead by hand until mixture sticks together.) If mixture is too soft to shape, wrap in plastic wrap and refrigerate for about 1 hour.

Roll nut paste into 1-inch balls; set 1 inch apart on wax paper–lined rimmed baking pans, pressing balls down to flatten bottoms slightly.

In the top of a double boiler over simmering water or in a small pan over lowest possible heat, stir chocolate chips just until melted. Dip each ball (by hand) into chocolate to cover top half; return to paper-lined pan, chocolate side up. Refrigerate, uncovered, until chocolate is set (about 30 minutes). If made ahead, cover and refrigerate for up to 1 week; let stand at room temperature for about 15 minutes before serving. Makes 3 to 4 dozen.

Spiced Milk

10   cups milk

 3   thin strips orange peel (orange part only), **each** about 4 inches long

 2   cinnamon sticks, **each** 3 to 4 inches long

In a 3- to 4-quart pan, combine milk, orange peel and cinnamon sticks. Heat over low heat, uncovered, stirring occasionally, until warm (do not boil). Makes 10 servings.

From the land of "let's pretend" comes this high-spirited Christmas party just for children. *A quirky caterpillar sandwich is surrounded by candy canes, popcorn "snowflakes," and plump, chocolaty sugarplums. Add festive cups of warm spiced milk, and watch your group of hungry youngsters eat it all up!*

Festive Dessert Buffet

Dazzle your holiday guests with a sweet-lover's dream: a sumptuous buffet that's *all* desserts.

The star of the show is Bûche de Noël—the traditional French Yule log, a rolled chocolate sponge cake filled and frosted with mocha buttercream. Offer two other cakes as well: a date and apricot fruitcake and a walnut torte layered with jam and whipped cream. Add our simple Chocolate Truffles and an array of pretty party cookies, and you have a selection that's sure to tempt any sweet tooth.

Our menu easily serves up to 24 guests. You can bake and freeze all the cookies well ahead of time. Make the fruitcake at least a few days or up to 2 months ahead; its flavor mellows as it ages. The Bûche de Noël can be completed a day in advance; for a party of 24, you'll need to make two bûches (each serves about 12).

Sparkling cranberry cocktail and good hot coffee help balance the sweetness of the desserts—but if you want to go all out for richness, try our Praline Eggnog (or keep it in mind for another holiday get-together).

MENU
Bûche de Noël
Western Fruitcake
Walnut-Rum Torte
Red & Green Apples
Finnish Ribbon Cakes (page 9)
Spritz (page 8)
Swedish Ginger Thins (page 19)
Almond Crescents (page 5)
Chocolate Truffles
Sparkling Cranberry
Blush Cocktail
Coffee   Praline Eggnog

Bûche de Noël
(Make 2 for the party)

6   large eggs, separated
¾   cup sugar
6   ounces semisweet chocolate, melted and cooled
    Basic Cooked Buttercream (recipe follows)
1½ teaspoons instant coffee granules or powder
¼   cup unsweetened cocoa or ⅓ cup ground sweet chocolate
¼   cup boiling water
    Holly leaves
    Red candied cherries

Butter a rimmed 10- by 15-inch baking pan, line with wax paper, and butter paper. Set aside.

In large bowl of an electric mixer, beat egg yolks and sugar until thick and lemon-colored. Blend in melted chocolate. Using clean, dry beaters, beat egg whites until they hold moist, distinct peaks; gently fold into chocolate mixture.

Pour batter into prepared pan; spread evenly. Bake in a 350° oven until surface of cake looks dry (12 to 14 minutes). Let cool in pan for 5 minutes, then turn out onto a large dishtowel. Peel off wax paper; trim off edges of cake. Place towel and cake on a large rack; let cool.

To fill and frost roll, set aside ½ cup of the buttercream. In a small bowl, stir together coffee, cocoa, and boiling water until smooth. Blend coffee mixture into remaining buttercream.

Spread cake with about half this mocha buttercream. Lift edge of cloth on a short end of cake, then gently guide cake into a smooth, tight roll. Refrigerate, wrapped in cloth, until chilled. Then unwrap and place on a serving tray, seam side down.

Neatly spread ends of log with reserved plain buttercream. Frost log with remaining mocha buttercream; lightly stroke icing the length of the log with the tines of a fork or tip of a knife to create a barklike pattern, swirling here and there to make "knots." Draw a tree-ring pattern on the ends of the log with a wooden pick dipped in a little of the mocha buttercream.

Decorate with a cluster of holly leaves and candied cherries. Refrigerate for at least 3 hours before serving. Makes about 12 servings.

Basic Cooked Buttercream. In small bowl of an electric mixer, beat 5 large **egg yolks** until thick and lemon-colored. Set aside. In a pan, blend ¾ cup **sugar** and ¼ cup **water**. Bring to a boil over high heat; then boil until syrup registers 232°F on a candy thermometer (syrup will spin a thread). Pour hot syrup into egg yolks in a thin, steady stream, beating constantly. Add 1 cup (½ lb.) **butter** (at room temperature); continue to beat until mixture is cool and fluffy. Cover and refrigerate until thick enough to spread well or for up to 3 weeks; stir well before using. Makes about 2½ cups.

Western Fruitcake
(Make 1 or 2 for the party)

1   package (8 oz.) pitted dates, quartered
2   cups quartered dried apricots
1   cup golden raisins
1   cup **each** whole blanched almonds and walnut pieces

1 cup green or red candied
  cherries
³/₁ cup **each** all-purpose
  flour and sugar
½ teaspoon baking powder
3 large eggs
1 teaspoon vanilla
  Rum or brandy
  (optional)

Butter a 5- by 9-inch loaf pan; line
with baking parchment or wax paper,
then butter paper. Set pan aside.

In a large bowl, combine dates,
apricots, raisins, almonds, walnuts,
and cherries. In another bowl, stir
together flour, sugar, and baking
powder; add to fruit mixture and
mix evenly.

Beat together eggs and vanilla.
Stir thoroughly into fruit mixture.
Spoon batter into prepared pan and
spread evenly; press batter into
corners of pan.

Bake in a 300° oven until golden
brown (about 1½ hours). Let cool in
pan on a rack for 10 minutes, then
turn out of pan. Peel off paper and let
cake cool on rack.

Wrap in foil; refrigerate for at least
2 days or up to 2 months before serving. If desired, sprinkle top of cake
with 1 tablespoon rum or brandy
once a week. Makes 1 loaf.

Walnut-Rum Torte
(Make 1 or 2 for the party)

2 cups walnut pieces or
  whole blanched almonds
⅓ cup all-purpose flour
1 teaspoon baking powder
¼ teaspoon salt
12 large eggs, separated
1⅓ cups sugar
1½ cups whipping cream
  About ½ cup rum
  (optional)
  About 1 cup raspberry
  jam
  About ½ cup chopped
  walnuts or almonds

In a blender or food processor,
whirl the 2 cups walnuts until finely
ground, using on-off pulses; be care-

This luscious array of sweets *is as pretty as it is delicious. Shown
(clockwise from top) are Walnut-Rum Torte, traditional Bûche de Noël,
chocolate-dipped Spritz cookies, Western Fruitcake, Almond Crescents
and Finnish Ribbon Cakes, additional Spritz cookies and Swedish Ginger
Thins, and glorious Chocolate Truffles.*

ful not to overgrind. Mix ground nuts with flour, baking powder, and salt; set aside.

In large bowl of an electric mixer, beat egg whites on high speed until foamy. Gradually add ¼ cup of the sugar and beat just until whites hold moist peaks (about 2 minutes).

In another large bowl, beat egg yolks on high speed until thick and lemon-colored. Gradually add ¾ cup of the sugar, beating until mixture holds soft peaks (about 8 minutes). Sprinkle nut mixture over beaten yolks and fold to blend; then gently fold in beaten whites.

Divide batter equally between 2 buttered, flour-dusted 9-inch cheesecake pans (at least 3 inches deep) with removable bottoms. Bake in a 350° oven until cakes spring back when gently pressed in center and begin to pull slightly from pan sides (about 35 minutes). Remove from oven and let cool thoroughly in pans on racks.

Run a knife around pan sides; then carefully remove sides. With a sharp serrated knife, trim off uneven and rough edges. Cut layers in half horizontally. In a bowl, beat cream with remaining ⅓ cup sugar until it holds stiff peaks; set aside.

Cut a 9-inch cardboard circle and cover it with foil. Place 1 of the layers, cut side up, on foil-covered circle. Spoon about 2 tablespoons of rum (if used) evenly over cake layer; spread about ⅓ cup of raspberry jam over layer, then spread ¼ of whipped cream over jam.

Place a second layer of cake on top of whipped cream. Repeat layering with rum, jam, and whipped cream. Top with another layer of cake. Continue until all layers are stacked; place top cake layer cut side down.

Spread top of cake with remaining whipped cream; sprinkle with chopped walnuts. Cut into wedges to serve. Makes 12 to 16 servings.

Chocolate Truffles

12 ounces semisweet chocolate, coarsely chopped
6 tablespoons whipping cream
   About 6 tablespoons unsweetened cocoa or ground sweet chocolate

Place chocolate and cream in a 2- to 3-quart pan over lowest possible heat. (If heat is too high, chocolate will separate.) Stir constantly until chocolate is melted and well blended with cream. Cover and refrigerate just until mixture is firm enough to hold its shape (about 40 minutes).

Spread cocoa on a small plate or a piece of wax paper. Using your fingers or 2 spoons, quickly shape about 1 teaspoon of the chocolate mixture at a time into a ball; then roll in cocoa until completely coated. Arrange in a single layer in a container. Cover and refrigerate until firm or for up to 2 weeks; serve at room temperature. Makes 2 to 2½ dozen.

Praline Eggnog

1¼ cups sugar
6 cups milk
3 cinnamon sticks, **each** about 3 inches long
1 vanilla bean (about 7 inches long), split in half lengthwise
2 cups whipping cream
12 large eggs
   Ground nutmeg

In a 3- to 4-quart pan, melt half the sugar over high heat, stirring constantly until it is a golden liquid; lumps will melt as you stir. Do not let syrup scorch. Remove from heat; at

once add milk, cinnamon sticks, and vanilla bean (mixture will sputter).

Return pan to medium heat and stir until caramelized sugar is dissolved. Cover and refrigerate until cold (at least 3 hours) or until next day. Remove spices. Rinse vanilla bean; reserve for other uses.

Beat cream until it holds soft peaks; set aside. Beat eggs with remaining sugar until about tripled in volume. Using a wire whisk, blend eggs and half the cream into caramelized milk. Pour into a 4- to 5-quart punch bowl, top with remaining cream, and sprinkle with nutmeg. Serve cold. Makes 24 servings, about ⅔ cup each.

Sparkling Cranberry Blush Cocktail

   About 1⅓ cups thawed frozen cranberry juice concentrate
4 bottles (about 25 oz. **each**) or 3 quarts sparkling apple juice or cider, chilled
12 thin lemon slices, halved

Pour cranberry concentrate and apple juice into a punch bowl or several pitchers. Ladle into punch cups or pour into champagne glasses; garnish each serving with a lemon. Makes 24 servings, ½ cup each.

Christmas Eve Family Supper

A cozy and comforting oven-baked meal reflects the spirit of a close-knit family Christmas Eve. The aroma of baking polenta and sausage fills the kitchen while you put together a simple green salad. For an extra-special dessert, make Chestnut Clouds—meringues topped with chestnut cream, served atop orange-scented custard. Or, if you prefer a simpler finale, offer a refreshing lemon sorbet and your favorite purchased or homemade cookies.

MENU

Oven Polenta & Baked Sausage with Sweet Red Peppers & Mushrooms
Sicilian Green Salad
Chestnut Clouds
Chianti or Gewürztraminer
Sparkling Water with Lemon

Oven Polenta & Baked Sausage with Sweet Red Peppers & Mushrooms

5   large red bell peppers, stemmed, seeded, and cut into large slices
3/4 pound mushrooms, thickly sliced
1 1/2 to 2 pounds mild or hot Italian sausages
5   cups regular-strength chicken broth
1 1/2 cups polenta (Italian-style cornmeal) or yellow cornmeal
1   small onion, chopped
1/4 cup (1/8 lb.) butter or margarine, cut into small pieces
2   cups (8 oz.) shredded jack cheese

Spread bell peppers and mushrooms in an even layer in a shallow 9- by 13-inch oval or rectangular baking dish. Lay sausages on vegetables. Bake in a 350° oven until sausages are lightly browned and no longer pink in center (cut to test), about 50 to 60 minutes; after 10 to 15 minutes, stir vegetables to moisten with pan drippings.

Meanwhile, in another shallow 9- by 13-inch rectangular or oval baking dish, stir together broth, polenta, onion, and butter. Place in oven alongside sausage mixture. Bake, uncovered, until liquid is absorbed (45 to 50 minutes). Remove polenta from oven and sprinkle with cheese.

Serve polenta, sausages, and vegetables from baking dishes; or, if desired, transfer to a large platter. Makes 4 to 6 servings.

Sicilian Green Salad

1   head romaine, rinsed and patted dry
2   oranges, peeled, white membranes removed
1   can (2 1/4 oz.) sliced ripe olives, drained well
1/4 cup orange juice
2   teaspoons red wine vinegar
1/2 teaspoon salt
1/4 teaspoon paprika
1/4 cup olive oil or salad oil

Tear romaine into bite-size pieces and place in a large bowl. Thinly slice oranges crosswise; place oranges and olives atop romaine. In a jar, combine orange juice, vinegar, salt, paprika, and oil; shake to blend well. Pour over salad and toss lightly to coat. Makes 6 servings.

Chestnut Clouds

4   large eggs, separated
2/3 cup sugar
1   teaspoon vanilla
2   cups milk
2   tablespoons orange-flavored liqueur
1/2 teaspoon grated orange peel
1/4 teaspoon cream of tartar
1/2 cup whipping cream
1   small can (about 8 3/4 oz., or 3/4 cup) chestnut spread
    Thin strands of orange peel

Place egg yolks in top of a double boiler with 1/3 cup of the sugar and vanilla; mix thoroughly. In a 1- to 2-quart pan, bring milk to scalding over medium-high heat; gradually stir into egg mixture. Place double boiler over simmering water and cook, stirring constantly, until custard coats a metal spoon in a smooth, velvety layer (10 to 15 minutes). Stir over ice water to cool. Stir in liqueur and grated orange peel. If made ahead, cover and refrigerate for up to 1 day.

In large bowl of an electric mixer, combine egg whites and cream of tartar; beat until foamy. Gradually add remaining 1/3 cup sugar and beat until mixture holds stiff, moist peaks. Bring about 1 inch of water just to simmering in a 10- to 12-inch frying pan over medium heat. Reduce heat so bubbles do not break the surface. With a large spoon and spatula, shape meringue into 5 or 6 large oval mounds and slide as many as will fit into pan of water. Cook, turning once, until meringues feel set when lightly touched (about 4 minutes). With a slotted spoon, lift out and drain on a rack. Blot off excess moisture with a paper towel. Repeat to cook remaining meringues. If made ahead, cover lightly and refrigerate for up to 1 day.

Shortly before serving, beat cream until it holds stiff peaks. Fold in chestnut spread. Pour equal portions of custard sauce into 5 or 6 rimmed dessert plates. Set a meringue on top of each; mound chestnut cream over meringues. Garnish with thin strands of orange peel. Makes 5 or 6 servings.

Christmas Morning Breakfast

On Christmas morning, wake up to a satisfying traditional breakfast that's as festive as it is easy to put together. Start the meal with chilled orange juice and champagne; then offer scrambled eggs, sautéed sliced ham, and warm Christmas bread filled with nuts and candied cherries. Alongside, provide a basket or pretty plate of juicy winter pears, apples, oranges, or other fruit in season. Freshly brewed coffee is always welcome, of course—but to make the breakfast as special as the occasion, serve mugs of our cinnamon-spiced New Mexican Hot Chocolate as well.

Only the sweet yeast bread requires advance preparation. You can bake it up to a month ahead and freeze, then reheat it.

MENU

Orange Juice   Champagne
Cherry-Almond
Christmas Wreath
Butter
Sautéed Ham Slices
Scrambled Eggs
Fresh Fruit in Season
New Mexican Hot Chocolate
Coffee

Cherry-Almond Christmas Wreath

1   *package active dry yeast*
¼   *cup warm water (about 110°F)*
½   *cup warm milk (about 110°F)*
3   *tablespoons sugar*
¼   *cup (⅛ lb.) butter or margarine, at room temperature*

1½   *teaspoons salt*
½   *teaspoon ground cardamom*
2   *large eggs*
1   *teaspoon grated lemon peel*
    About 3½ cups all-purpose flour
    Cherry-Almond Filling (recipe follows)
    Sugar Glaze (recipe follows)

In large bowl of an electric mixer, sprinkle yeast over water and let stand for about 5 minutes to soften. Stir in milk, sugar, butter, salt, cardamom, eggs, and lemon peel. Beat in 2 cups of the flour, a cup at a time. Then beat on medium speed for 3 minutes, scraping bowl frequently.

If using a dough hook, beat in enough of the remaining flour (about 1¼ cups) to make a soft dough. *If mixing by hand,* stir in about 1¼ cups flour with a heavy spoon, mixing to make a soft dough.

Scrape dough out onto a floured board and knead until smooth (5 to 10 minutes), adding more flour as needed to prevent sticking. Place dough in a greased bowl; turn over to grease top. Cover and let rise in a warm place until doubled (about 1½ hours).

Punch dough down and knead briefly on a floured board to release air. Then roll into a 9- by 30-inch rectangle. Crumble Cherry-Almond Filling and scatter it over dough to within 1 inch of edges. Starting with a long side, roll up dough tightly, jelly roll fashion. Moisten edge with water; pinch to seal.

Using a floured sharp knife, cut roll in half lengthwise; carefully turn cut sides up. Loosely twist half-rolls around each other, keeping cut sides up. Carefully transfer to a greased and flour-dusted 12- by 15-inch baking sheet and shape into a 10-inch circle; pinch ends together firmly to seal. Let rise, uncovered, in a warm place until puffy (45 to 60 minutes).

Bake in a 375° oven until lightly browned (about 20 minutes). Run wide spatulas under wreath to loosen; then transfer to a rack. Drizzle glaze over wreath while still warm.

If made ahead, do not glaze; let cool on a rack, then wrap airtight and hold at room temperature for up to 24 hours or freeze for up to 1 month (thaw unwrapped). To reheat, wrap in foil; place in a 350° oven until heated through (about 15 minutes). Makes 1 large wreath.

Cherry-Almond Filling. In large bowl of an electric mixer, beat ¼ cup (⅛ lb.) **butter** or margarine (at room temperature), ¼ cup **all-purpose flour**, and 2 tablespoons **sugar** until smooth. Stir in ⅔ cup finely chopped **blanched almonds**, ¼ cup *each* chopped **red and green candied cherries**, ½ teaspoon grated **lemon peel**, and ¾ teaspoon **almond extract**. Cover and refrigerate.

Sugar Glaze. In a small bowl, blend ⅔ cup **powdered sugar**, 1½ teaspoons **lemon juice**, and 1 tablespoon **water** until smooth.

New Mexican Hot Chocolate

4   *cups milk*
3   *cinnamon sticks, **each** about 3 inches long*
6   *ounces bittersweet or semisweet chocolate, broken into pieces*
⅓   *cup slivered almonds*
2   *tablespoons sugar*

In a 2-quart pan, combine milk and cinnamon sticks. Warm over low heat, stirring occasionally. Meanwhile, combine chocolate, almonds, and sugar in a blender. Whirl until a coarse powder forms.

Increase heat under milk to high; stir milk until it's just at the boiling point. Lift out cinnamon sticks and set aside. Pour half the milk into blender; cover (hold on lid with a thick towel) and whirl to combine. Pour in remaining milk and whirl until blended. Split cinnamon sticks lengthwise into halves; put a section in each of 6 mugs and fill with hot, foamy chocolate. Makes 6 servings.

Celebrate Christmas morning *with a festive breakfast that features a luscious sweet bread wreath, tender scrambled eggs, fresh fruit and juicy ham slices. To drink, offer hot spiced chocolate and "a bit of bubbly," too.*

Christmas Day Feasts

■

Christmas Day is finally here, and it's time to bring family and guests together around a festive holiday table. Create a feast worthy of the occasion—like this lavish Roast Pork Dinner (see page 88)—from any of the sumptuous menus in this chapter.

Roast Turkey Dinner

(Pictured on page 83)

"Turkey with all the trimmings" is deliciously updated in this impressive Christmas Day dinner for 10 guests. An elegant radicchio-shrimp salad leads up to the star attraction— a whole boned turkey filled with savory rice-sausage stuffing. Spicy plum sauce, butter-steamed peas, and an unusual carrot-parsnip tart complement the golden turkey; wine-poached pears with a tangy Stilton custard finish the feast in grand style.

Ask your butcher to bone the turkey for you—or do it yourself, following our simple instructions.

MENU

Radicchio, Shrimp & Dill Salad
Boned Turkey with Rice &
Sausage Stuffing
Chinese Plum Sauce
Carrot-Parsnip Tart
Peas with Lettuce
Port-poached Pears
with Stilton Custard

Radicchio, Shrimp & Dill Salad

2   heads radicchio, **each** 4
    to 4½ inches in diameter

2   to 3 tablespoons slivered
    prosciutto, Black Forest
    or Westphalian ham, or
    dry salami

½   cup olive oil or salad oil

1   pound cooked, shelled,
    deveined medium-size
    shrimp (30 to 36 per lb.)

3   tablespoons red wine
    vinegar

2   to 3 tablespoons chopped
    fresh dill
    Salt and white pepper
    Dill sprigs

Cut core from each head of radicchio. Run cold water through cored

center; remove 10 of the largest leaves (save remaining leaves for another salad). Wrap leaves in paper towels and enclose in a plastic bag, then refrigerate to crisp (at least 2 hours) or for up to 3 days.

In a 1- to 2-quart pan, combine ham and oil. Warm over low heat, uncovered, until oil picks up ham flavor (about 10 minutes). Let cool.

In a bowl, mix oil-ham mixture, shrimp, vinegar, and chopped dill. Season to taste with salt and white pepper. (At this point, you may cover and refrigerate for up to 1 day.)

To serve, place 1 radicchio leaf on each of 10 salad plates. Mound shrimp mixture equally in leaves; garnish with dill sprigs. Makes 10 servings.

Boned Turkey with Rice & Sausage Stuffing

1   turkey (10 to 12 lbs.),
    thawed if frozen
    Rice & Sausage
    Stuffing (recipe follows)
    Salad oil
    Salt and pepper

Begin by boning turkey. First, remove giblets and neck; reserve for your favorite giblet gravy. Release legs if trussed (held with skin or wire). Rinse bird, drain, and pat dry.

Turn turkey breast down. With a small, sharp knife, cut through to backbone from neck to tail. Holding tip of knife parallel to bone, cut and scrape meat from carcass, pulling flesh and skin back as you cut; take care not to pierce skin.

For each side, first follow contours of back, working toward breast. Slide knife tip along ribs to wing socket. Carefully cut tendons around joint. When joint is well exposed, press back on wing to snap loose. Guide knife along shoulder blade and wishbone to cut free.

Next, follow contours of back to hip socket. Cut hip socket free in the same way as for wings. Cut down toward breastbone around the ribs to cartilage and keel. Then, gently pulling and cutting, separate keel and

cartilage from breast. Lift out carcass (use to make broth, if desired). Pull off and discard lumps of fat. Cover bird and refrigerate until ready to stuff or until next day.

When ready to roast turkey, lay bird out flat, skin side down. Mound dressing onto center of bird, shaping dressing to resemble the missing carcass. Lift edges of back over rice, overlapping skin slightly; secure with small skewers. Pull neck skin over back; skewer. Fold wingtips over back.

Gently turn turkey over, rub lightly with oil, and carefully place on a V-shaped rack in a 12- by 14-inch roasting pan.

Roast, uncovered, in a 350° oven until a meat thermometer inserted in thickest part of thigh on inside of leg registers 175°F—2 to 2½ hours. (Since optimum temperatures for breast at center and thigh are 170°F and 185°F, respectively, and both cook at the same rate, we suggest 175°F as the best compromise.)

Remove turkey from oven and let rest on rack for at least 30 minutes. Carefully transfer bird to a large carving board. To serve, cut bird in half lengthwise with a very sharp knife. Remove skewers, then lay each half cut side down. Slice off wings; then, using leg to anchor bird, slice breast halves diagonally to include some dressing with each serving. Cut off thighs and separate drumsticks, then slice meat from thighs. Season to taste with salt and pepper. Makes 10 to 12 servings.

Rice & Sausage Stuffing. In a 3- to 4-quart pan, combine 2½ cups **pearl rice**, 3 cups **regular-strength chicken broth**, 1 teaspoon *each* **rubbed sage** and **dry thyme leaves**, and ½ teaspoon **dry rosemary**. Cover and bring to a boil over high heat. Reduce heat to low; cook without stirring until liquid is absorbed (about 15 minutes).

Remove casings from 1½ pounds **mild Italian sausages** and crumble meat into a 10- to 12-inch frying pan. Cook over medium-high heat, stirring occasionally to break up big chunks, until meat is lightly browned and no longer pink in center (cut to test). Add ½ cup **raisins**; stir often until raisins puff. With a slotted spoon, lift out meat and raisins and add to rice; let cool.

Rinse and drain ¾ pound **mustard greens**. Cut off coarse stems; discard. Chop greens; add to sausage drippings. Cook over medium-high heat, stirring often, until leaves are wilted, bright green, and beginning to brown (about 8 minutes). Add greens, drippings, and 1 (about 5 oz.) grated **Parmesan cheese** to rice; mix. If made ahead, cover and refrigerate until next day.

Chinese Plum Sauce

2 cans (1 lb. **each**) plums in heavy syrup

¾ cup water

1 tablespoon salad oil
Spice Mixture
(recipe follows)

½ cup tomato sauce

1 medium-size onion, chopped

1 tablespoon **each** soy sauce and Worcestershire

¼ teaspoon liquid hot pepper seasoning

1 tablespoon rice vinegar or wine vinegar

Drain plums, reserving 1¼ cups syrup (discard remaining syrup). Remove pits from plums; then whirl plums, water, and reserved 1¼ cups syrup in a blender until puréed. Set aside.

Heat oil in a 3- to 4-quart pan over medium-high heat; stir Spice Mixture into hot oil. Add plum purée, tomato sauce, onion, soy, Worcestershire, and hot pepper seasoning. Boil, uncovered, stirring often, until reduced to 3 cups (about 25 minutes). Stir in vinegar. Serve

warm, or cover and refrigerate for up to 3 weeks. Makes 3 cups.

Spice Mixture. Blend 1 teaspoon **Chinese five-spice** (or ¼ teaspoon *each* ground cinnamon, cloves, ginger, and anise seeds); ½ teaspoon *each* **ground cinnamon**, **ground cumin**, and **dry mustard**; and ¼ teaspoon **pepper**.

Carrot-Parsnip Tart

Press-in Pastry
(recipe follows)

2 cups **each** shredded peeled carrots and parsnips

½ cup water

3 large eggs

1½ teaspoons grated orange peel

1 teaspoon grated lemon peel

2 tablespoons all-purpose flour

⅔ cup sugar

1 cup lemon-flavored yogurt

½ cup pecan halves

Evenly press pastry over bottom and sides of a 9-inch tart pan with a removable bottom. Bake in a 325° oven until pale gold (15 to 20 minutes). Remove from oven.

While crust is baking, place carrots, parsnips, and water in a 10- to 12-inch frying pan. Bring to a boil over high heat; then reduce heat to low, cover, and simmer, stirring occasionally, until vegetables are very soft to bite and liquid has evaporated (about 12 minutes). Remove from heat and let cool.

In a bowl, whisk eggs, orange peel, lemon peel, flour, sugar, and yogurt until blended. Stir in carrots and parsnips. Pour mixture into tart shell. Evenly arrange pecans on top in a double row around rim. Bake in a 325° oven until tart no longer jiggles in center when pan is gently shaken (40 to 45 minutes).

Let cool on a rack for at least 10 minutes; or let cool completely, then cover and refrigerate until next day. Run a knife between crust and pan

rim before serving, then remove rim. Makes 10 servings.

Press-in Pastry. In a food processor or a bowl, combine 1 cup **all-purpose flour** and 3 tablespoons **sugar**. Add ⅓ cup firm **butter** or margarine, cut into small pieces; whirl or rub with your fingers until fine crumbs form. Add 1 large **egg yolk**; process or stir with a fork until dough holds together when pressed.

Peas with Lettuce

6 tablespoons butter or margarine

4 cups shredded iceberg lettuce

2 packages (1 lb. **each**) frozen tiny peas, thawed, drained well

6 tablespoons lightly packed minced parsley

¾ teaspoon sugar

¼ teaspoon ground nutmeg
Salt

Melt butter in a 12-inch frying pan over high heat. Add lettuce and cook, stirring, until wilted (2 to 3 minutes). Immediately stir in peas, parsley, sugar, and nutmeg. Cook until peas are heated through and juices are boiling. Season to taste with salt. Makes 10 servings.

Port-poached Pears with Stilton Custard

4½ cups port

1 cup plus 6 tablespoons sugar

10 firm-ripe pears (stems left on), peeled

3 large egg yolks

1 cup milk

⅔ cup crumbled Stilton cheese, at room temperature

½ teaspoon vanilla
Shredded orange or lemon peel (optional)

Holiday turkey—*boned and shaped around a rice stuffing—takes on an elegant new look in our savory Roast Turkey Dinner. Equally original accompaniments include a radicchio-shrimp salad, a tasty carrot-parsnip tart, tiny peas, and spoonfuls of spicy plum sauce. Richly sauced poached pears provide the finishing touch.*

In an 8-quart pan or a 12-inch frying pan with a domed lid, bring port and 1 cup of the sugar to a boil over high heat. Lay pears on their sides in pan. Then reduce heat, cover, and simmer until pears are tender when pierced (10 to 15 minutes); gently turn pears over halfway through cooking. Lift pears from syrup and transfer to a large bowl.

Boil syrup over high heat, uncovered, until reduced to 1¼ cups (20 to 25 minutes). Pour over pears and let cool. Cover and refrigerate until cold (at least 2 hours) or until next day; turn pears over in syrup after 1 hour.

In a bowl, lightly whisk together egg yolks and remaining 6 tablespoons sugar. Pour milk into top of a double boiler; place directly over medium heat and bring milk to scalding, stirring often. Gradually whisk milk into yolks and sugar. Return mixture to top of double boiler.

Set top of double boiler in place over simmering water. Cook, stirring constantly, until custard is thick enough to coat the back of a metal spoon (about 10 minutes). Immediately add cheese; stir just until cheese is melted. Remove from heat and stir in vanilla. Let cool, then cover and refrigerate until cold (at least 4 hours) or until next day.

To serve, turn pears over in syrup, then lift from syrup and set aside. Carefully spoon syrup on 1 side of each of 10 rimmed dessert plates, dividing equally. Then spoon cheese custard equally on other side of plates. Lay 1 pear atop syrup and custard on each plate; garnish with orange peel, if desired. Makes 10 servings.

Roast Goose Dinner

(Pictured on page 86)

Bring the spirit of Dickensian England to your holiday table with this Christmas feast for eight. The meal centers around a golden, crisp-skinned roast goose, served with port wine sauce and tender poached apples and prunes. And for dessert, there's a traditional steamed pudding —flamed with brandy, garnished with holly, and crowned with a fluffy, vanilla-scented whipped cream sauce.

To offset the richness of meat and pudding, we've selected a trio of lighter accompaniments. The first course is simply cooked, chilled leek halves, topped with tiny shrimp and a tangy mustard-lemon sauce. Citrus flavors stand out in the yam casserole, too—it's a combination of yam, orange, and onion slices, accented with honey and almonds. Bright, savory spinach-stuffed tomatoes add Christmas color as well as fresh flavor to the meal.

Though this menu is lavish and varied, it doesn't require you to spend all Christmas Day in the kitchen. The leeks and yam casserole can be prepared a day ahead; you can wash the spinach for the stuffed tomatoes the day before, too. The pudding can be steamed up to 2 weeks before Christmas and stored in the freezer. The day of the feast, you can devote your attention to roasting the goose.

A final note: Though you may be able to buy fresh geese during the holiday season, they're usually sold frozen. Fresh or frozen, these birds are often a special-order item. Unless you live near a supplier carrying frozen geese in stock all year round, be sure to order well in advance.

MENU

Chilled Leeks & Shrimp
Roast Goose with
Giblet Wine Sauce
Port-poached Fruit
Layered Yam Casserole
Spinach-stuffed Tomatoes
Persimmon Pudding

Chilled Leeks & Shrimp

8   leeks, **each** about 1 inch in diameter
½   cup whipping cream
¾   cup mayonnaise
1½   tablespoons lemon juice
3   tablespoons Dijon mustard
     Salt and pepper
8   romaine leaves
¾   to 1 pound small cooked shrimp

Trim and discard leek roots and all but about 1½ inches of dark green leaves. Discard tough outer leaves. Cut leeks in half lengthwise; rinse each half under cold running water, separating layers to wash out dirt.

Place leek halves in a single layer in a wide frying pan; add water to cover. (If pan won't hold all the leeks at once, cook in 2 batches.) Bring water to a boil over high heat; reduce heat, cover, and simmer until stem ends are tender when pierced (5 to 7 minutes). Lift out leeks; let cool, then cover and refrigerate until next day.

In a small bowl, beat cream until it holds soft peaks. Combine mayonnaise, lemon juice, and mustard; fold in cream. Season to taste with salt and pepper. (At this point, you may cover and refrigerate for up to 6 hours.)

Just before serving, arrange romaine leaves on 8 individual plates or on a serving platter. Place 2 leek halves on each leaf and distribute shrimp evenly over leeks. Pass dressing at the table. Makes 8 servings.

Roast Goose with Giblet Wine Sauce

1   goose (11 to 13 lbs.), thawed if frozen
     Giblet Wine Sauce (recipe follows)
     Parsley sprigs (optional)
     Shredded orange peel (optional)

Remove goose giblets and reserve for sauce. Pull out and discard lumps of fat in neck and body cavities. Rinse bird with cold water, drain, and pat dry. With a fork, prick skin at ½-inch intervals in thigh and lower breast areas. Turn bird breast down and fasten neck skin to back with a skewer. Tie drumsticks together or tuck them into the loose skin at bottom of cavity.

Place goose, breast down, on a rack in a large roasting pan (at least 11 by 17 inches). Roast, uncovered, in a 400° oven for 1 hour. Every 30 minutes, ladle out fat accumulating in roasting pan (or siphon out with a bulb baster); reserve 2 tablespoons for sauce. Discard remaining fat or save for other cooking uses. Meanwhile, prepare stock for Giblet Wine Sauce (recipe follows).

After goose has roasted for 1 hour, reduce oven temperature to 325°. Protecting your hands, turn goose breast up on rack and insert a meat thermometer into thickest part

---

of breast (not touching bone). Continue to roast, siphoning fat from pan every 30 minutes, until thermometer registers 175°F—about 1½ more hours for an 11-pound bird, about 2 more hours for a 13-pounder.

Lift goose from roasting pan, remove skewers and string (if used), and place bird breast up on a platter. Keep warm while you prepare Giblet Wine Sauce and Port-poached Fruit.

Surround goose with poached fruit; garnish with parsley and orange peel, if desired. Present at the table.

To carve, cut off tips and first joints of wings. Holding remaining wing section with fingers, sever from body by forcing knife through side of breast into joint while twisting wing.

To carve legs, turn goose breast side down and cut through back skin to expose joints next to center back. Anchor a fork firmly in thigh and press drumstick down to board; then cut between leg and body at joint. Repeat for other leg. Separate thighs and drumsticks at joints, then cut along bone to divide each into 2 pieces.

Remove each side of breast by sliding a knife between meat and keel bone. Cut down to breastbone along wishbone and around to wing joint. Cut meat free in 1 piece; thinly slice each breast crosswise. Trim off any clinging pieces of meat from the carcass.

Serve sliced goose with Giblet Wine Sauce and Port-poached Fruit. Makes 8 to 10 servings.

Giblet Wine Sauce. Reserve goose liver for other uses. Chop remaining **goose giblets** and set aside. Pour 2 tablespoons **reserved goose fat** into a 2- to 3-quart pan and set over medium-high heat. Add giblets, cook, stirring, until well browned. Add 1 small **onion**, chopped; cook, stirring, until golden. Add 2 cups **water**; 1 **chicken bouillon cube**; 1 stalk **celery**, cut into pieces; 1 **bay leaf**; and ¼ teaspoon **dry thyme leaves**. Bring to a boil; then reduce heat, cover, and simmer for 1½ to 2 hours while goose roasts.

To **browned particles in roasting pan,** add hot giblet-vegetable mixture; scrape browned bits free. Pour mixture through a wire strainer into a 1- to 2-quart pan; discard residue. Boil liquid rapidly to reduce to 1¼ cups. Add ½ cup **port**; return to a boil. Season to taste with **salt** and **pepper**. Serve as is; or, if desired, thicken juices by stirring in 1½ tablespoons **cornstarch** mixed with 1½ tablespoons **water**. Stir until sauce boils and thickens (about 1 minute).

Port-poached Fruit

In a pan, heat 1½ cups **port** just until hot. Remove from heat, add 2 cups (one 12-oz. package) **pitted prunes**, and let stand for 10 minutes; then drain off port and reserve. Meanwhile, peel, core, and quarter 4 or 5 **Golden Delicious apples**.

In a wide frying pan, melt 2 tablespoons **butter** or margarine. Add apples and 2 tablespoons **lemon juice**; turn fruit to coat. Add port; cover and simmer over medium-low heat until apples begin to soften (about 4 minutes). Uncover; increase heat to high, add prunes, and cook, turning fruit frequently, until apples are translucent and sauce clings to fruit (about 2 minutes). Makes 8 to 10 servings.

Layered Yam Casserole

- 3½ to 4 pounds yams, scrubbed
- ¼ cup sliced almonds
- 1 large onion, thinly sliced
- 3 oranges
- ½ cup (¼ lb.) butter or margarine, melted
- 2 tablespoons honey
  Salt and pepper

In a 5- to 6-quart pan, bring 2 inches of water to a boil. Add yams; when water returns to a boil, reduce heat, cover pan, and cook until yams are tender when pierced (20 to 30 minutes). Drain and let cool; then peel and cut diagonally into ¼-inch-thick slices.

Spread almonds in a shallow baking pan and toast in a 350° oven until golden (about 8 minutes), shaking pan occasionally. Set aside. Arrange ⅓ of the yams in an even layer in a shallow 3-quart baking dish. Top with half the onion; then arrange half the remaining yams atop onion. Top with remaining onion and yams.

Remove and discard peel and all white membrane from 2 of the oranges; then slice oranges and arrange on top of yams. Squeeze juice from remaining orange and combine with butter and honey; pour evenly over yam mixture. Sprinkle lightly with salt and pepper. Cover with lid or foil. (At this point, you may refrigerate until next day.)

Sprinkle almonds over top of casserole and bake, covered, in a 325° oven for 45 minutes (55 minutes if refrigerated). Uncover; continue to bake until almonds are slightly crisped and casserole is heated through (about 5 more minutes). Makes 8 servings.

(Continued on next page)

In the tradition of a Victorian Christmas, *present a succulent golden roast goose with wine-poached fruit. The accompaniments—a chilled shrimp-and-leek starter, savory stuffed tomatoes, and an orange-scented yam casserole—add a light, fresh touch to the menu.*

Spinach-stuffed Tomatoes

8 medium-size tomatoes
1 tablespoon butter or margarine
1 tablespoon salad oil
1 medium-size onion, chopped
¾ pound spinach, rinsed well, coarsely chopped
1¼ cups (about 6¼ oz.) shredded Parmesan cheese
2 tablespoons fine dry bread crumbs
⅛ teaspoon ground nutmeg

Cut off the top fourth of each tomato; reserve for other uses, if desired. With a small spoon, scoop out pulp to make hollow shells. Chop pulp and place in a colander to drain.

Melt butter in oil in a wide frying pan over medium-high heat. Add onion and cook, stirring, until soft. Stir in drained tomato pulp and spinach and cook, stirring, until spinach is wilted (3 to 4 minutes). Stir in 1 cup of the cheese, bread crumbs, and nutmeg.

Fill tomatoes with spinach mixture and arrange in an ungreased baking pan; sprinkle evenly with remaining ¼ cup cheese. Broil 4 inches below heat until cheese is lightly browned (3 to 4 minutes). Makes 8 servings.

Persimmon Pudding

1½ cups **each** sugar and all-purpose flour
1½ teaspoons ground cinnamon
½ teaspoon ground nutmeg
1 tablespoon baking soda
3 tablespoons hot water
1½ cups ripe persimmon pulp
2 large eggs
1½ cups chopped pitted prunes
1 cup coarsely chopped almonds, walnuts, hazelnuts, or pistachio nuts
½ to ¾ cup brandy
2 teaspoons vanilla
1½ teaspoons lemon juice
¾ cup (⅜ lb.) butter or margarine, melted and cooled to lukewarm
Holly sprigs (optional)
Soft Sauce (recipe follows)

In a bowl, mix sugar, flour, cinnamon, and nutmeg. In a large bowl, stir together baking soda and hot water, then mix in persimmon pulp and eggs. Beat until blended. Add sugar mixture, prunes, almonds, ⅓ cup of the brandy, vanilla, lemon juice, and butter. Stir until evenly mixed.

Scrape batter into a buttered 9- to 10-cup pudding mold (either plain or tube-shaped) with lid or a deep 9- to 10-cup metal bowl. Cover tightly with lid or foil. Place on a rack in a deep 5- to 6-quart (or larger) pan. Add 1 inch of water, cover pan, and steam over medium heat until pudding is firm when lightly pressed in center (about 2¼ hours for tube mold, 2½ hours for plain mold). Add boiling water as needed to keep about 1 inch in pan.

Uncover pudding and let stand on a rack until slightly cooled (about 15 minutes). Invert onto a dish; lift off mold.

If made ahead, let cool completely. If desired, wrap pudding in a single layer of cheesecloth and moisten evenly with 3 to 4 tablespoons of the brandy. Wrap airtight in foil and refrigerate for up to 2 weeks; freeze for longer storage (thaw wrapped). To reheat, discard cheesecloth, wrap pudding in foil, and steam on a rack over 1 inch of boiling water in a covered 5- to 6-quart pan until hot (about 45 minutes).

Garnish pudding with holly, if desired. To flame pudding, warm 3 to 4 tablespoons brandy in a 2- to 4-cup pan until bubbly. Carefully ignite (not beneath a vent, fan, or flammable items) and pour over pudding. Slice and serve with Soft Sauce. Makes 8 servings.

Soft Sauce. Separate 2 large **eggs**. In a bowl, beat whites until they hold soft peaks; gradually beat in ½ cup **powdered sugar** until whites hold stiff peaks. In another bowl, using the same beaters, beat egg yolks with ½ cup **powdered sugar** and ½ teaspoon **vanilla** until very thick. Fold whites and yolks together. Serve; or cover and hold at room temperature for up to 2 hours (stir before serving). Makes about 2¼ cups.

Roast Pork Dinner

(Pictured on page 80)

As impressive as it is delicious, this roast pork dinner for 12 to 14 people features a succession of varied and mouthwatering courses, from a rich, creamy pistachio soup to a refreshing salad of fennel and watercress to the final triumph—a dessert trifle made with fresh oranges and chocolate. A zesty cranberry-pepper sauce gives the succulent pork roast an extra-special touch.

MENU

Cream of Pistachio Soup
Roast Pork
with Cranberry-Pepper Sauce
Mashed Potatoes & Broccoli
Minted Carrots
Fennel & Watercress Salad
Fresh Orange & Chocolate Trifle

Cream of Pistachio Soup

3	*cups shelled (6 cups or 1½ lbs. in shell) natural, roasted, or roasted salted pistachio nuts*
½	*cup (¼ lb.) butter or margarine*
1	*large onion, finely chopped*
1	*cup chopped celery*
2	*cloves garlic, minced or pressed*
⅓	*cup dry sherry*
2	*large cans (49½ oz. **each**) regular-strength chicken broth*
¾	*cup long-grain white rice*
4	*parsley sprigs*
1	*bay leaf*
2	*cups whipping cream Whole chives*

Rub off as much of the pistachio skins as possible, then set nuts aside. Melt butter in an 8-quart pan over medium heat; add onion, celery, and garlic. Cook, stirring, until onion is very soft but not browned (about 15 minutes); stir often.

Add sherry, 1½ cups of the pistachios, broth, rice, parsley, and bay leaf. Bring to a boil; then reduce heat, cover, and simmer until rice is tender to bite (about 30 minutes). Discard bay leaf.

Whirl soup in a food processor or blender, a portion at a time, until very smooth. Pour through a wire strainer and discard residue. Return soup to pan.

Add cream to soup and stir over medium-low heat until steaming (5 to 7 minutes). Pour into a tureen or individual bowls; garnish with whole chives and sprinkle with remaining 1½ cups pistachios. Makes 3½ quarts.

Roast Pork with Cranberry-Pepper Sauce

1	*can (1 lb.) whole berry cranberry sauce*
¼	*cup lemon juice*
1	*boned, rolled, and tied half leg of pork (5 to 7 lbs.) Salt and pepper*
3	*tablespoons canned green peppercorns, drained*
½	*teaspoon cracked black pepper*

To make cranberry-lemon baste, pour cranberry sauce into a wire strainer set over a bowl; let drain. Measure out ¼ cup of the cranberry liquid and combine with lemon juice. Stir any remaining cranberry liquid back into cranberry sauce; set sauce and baste aside.

Place pork, fat side up, on a rack in a roasting pan. Sprinkle lightly with salt and pepper. Roast, uncovered, in a 400° oven for 20 minutes, then reduce oven temperature to 325° and continue to roast until a meat thermometer inserted in the thickest part of roast registers 170°F—about 2

more hours for a 5-pound roast, about 2¾ more hours for a 7-pound roast (allow 24 to 28 minutes *total* per pound).

About halfway through cooking time, pour cranberry-lemon baste over meat, then baste meat with pan juices every 30 minutes until done.

When meat is done, transfer to a platter or board; keep warm. Skim and discard fat from pan juices and pour juices into a sauce boat. In a serving bowl, combine peppercorns, cranberry sauce, and cracked pepper. Serve meat with juices and cranberry sauce. Makes 12 to 14 servings.

Mashed Potatoes & Broccoli

5	*pounds russet potatoes*
2	*pounds broccoli*
6	*tablespoons butter or margarine*
½	*cup milk Salt and pepper*

Peel potatoes and cut into ½-inch cubes. Set aside. Cut off broccoli flowerets; peel stalks. Finely chop tender parts of stalks and all but a few flowerets; discard tough parts of stalks.

In an 8-quart pan, bring 4 quarts of water to a boil. Add potatoes, cover, and cook until tender when pierced (about 15 minutes). Add all broccoli and cook just until tender to bite (about 3 minutes). Don't overcook or broccoli will lose its bright color. Drain well, discarding water.

Remove whole flowerets from drained vegetables in pan. Add butter and milk to vegetables; stir over low heat until butter is melted. With a potato masher, mash vegetables smoothly. Season to taste with salt and pepper. Spoon vegetables into a warmed bowl; garnish with reserved whole broccoli flowerets. Makes 12 to 14 servings.

Minted Carrots

3 pounds carrots, peeled
¼ cup (⅛ lb.) butter or
   margarine
1 cup golden raisins
1 cup regular-strength
   chicken broth
½ cup firmly packed fresh
   mint sprigs
4 teaspoons firmly packed
   brown sugar
   Salt and pepper

Cut carrots into matchstick pieces about ¼ inch wide, ¼ inch thick, and 3 to 4 inches long.

Melt butter in a 12-inch frying pan over medium heat. Add carrots, raisins, broth, ¼ cup of the mint sprigs, and sugar. Bring to a boil; then reduce heat, cover, and simmer until carrots are tender-crisp to bite (about 10 minutes). Uncover and boil over high heat until liquid has evaporated (5 to 10 more minutes), shaking pan often and gently lifting and turning carrots with a spatula.

Meanwhile, strip leaves from all but 3 or 4 of remaining ¼ cup mint sprigs. Finely sliver leaves.

Discard cooked mint sprigs from carrot mixture; season carrots to taste with salt and pepper. Turn onto a warmed platter and sprinkle with slivered mint; garnish with mint sprigs. Makes 12 to 14 servings.

Fennel & Watercress Salad

1 pound watercress
4 large carrots, peeled and
   cut in half lengthwise
6 medium-size heads
   fennel (3 to 3½ lbs.
   total), ends trimmed to
   within 1 inch of bulb
6 ounces Parmesan cheese
1 cup olive oil or salad oil
½ cup white wine vinegar
1 tablespoon Dijon
   mustard
   Salt and pepper

Pluck off tender watercress sprigs to make 12 cups; rinse well, then wrap in paper towels and enclose in plastic bags. Refrigerate to crisp (about 30 minutes) or until next day.

With a vegetable peeler, evenly pare 50 to 60 long, thick, wide strips down length of carrots; reserve remaining parts of carrots for another use. Tightly curl carrot strips and place in ice water, wedging curls against ice cubes to preserve the curl; refrigerate for at least 15 minutes or up to 1 hour.

Trim any bruises from fennel; then cut heads into quarters lengthwise, remove and discard core and leaves. Thinly slice sections crosswise to make about 9 cups.

Cut cheese into very thin shavings with a cheese slicer or knife. Set aside.

Drain carrot curls on paper towels. In a large bowl, mix oil, vinegar, and mustard. Add carrots, fennel, and watercress; mix well. Arrange on a platter or 12 to 14 salad plates. Offer cheese, salt, and pepper to add to taste. Makes 12 to 14 servings.

Fresh Orange & Chocolate Trifle

1 cup sugar
½ cup water
1 vanilla bean (about
   6 inches long), split
   lengthwise; or
   ½ teaspoon vanilla
3 unpeeled thin-skinned
   oranges (3 to 4 inches in
   diameter), cut crosswise
   into ⅛-inch-thick slices
   and seeded
⅓ cup orange-flavored
   liqueur
3 ounces (½ cup) chopped
   semisweet or milk
   chocolate
1 cup whipping cream,
   whipped
   Pastry Cream
   (recipe follows)
1 purchased 9-inch sponge
   cake layer, torn into
   bite-size chunks
   Semisweet or milk
   chocolate curls

In a 10- to 12-inch frying pan, bring sugar, water, and vanilla bean to a boil (if using vanilla extract, add later, as directed). Add oranges; reduce heat and simmer, uncovered, stirring occasionally, until peel looks translucent (about 20 minutes). Lift out oranges and vanilla bean (reserve for Pastry Cream). Set aside.

Measure syrup in pan, adding any liquid that has accumulated with oranges. Boil to reduce to ⅔ cup, or add water to make ⅔ cup. Stir in liqueur, then vanilla (if used). Set aside.

Set aside 5 of the best-looking orange slices. Coarsely chop enough of the remaining slices to make ⅔ cup; set aside. Arrange all remaining slices, overlapping as needed, in bottom and slightly up sides of a wide 2- to 2½-quart glass bowl.

Gently fold the ⅔ cup chopped oranges, chopped chocolate, and whipped cream into Pastry Cream.

Ladle about ¼ of the cream mixture into orange-lined bowl and spread gently to cover oranges. Scatter about half the sponge cake pieces over cream. Slowly spoon half the reserved syrup over cake, letting it soak in. Repeat to make a second layer, using about ⅓ of the remaining cream mixture and all the remaining cake pieces and syrup. Spoon in remaining cream mixture, being sure to cover cake. Garnish with reserved orange slices and chocolate curls. Cover and refrigerate for at least 3 hours or until next day. To serve, spoon into dessert bowls. Makes 12 to 14 servings.

Pastry Cream. In a 2- to 3-quart pan, stir together ½ cup *each* **sugar** and **all-purpose flour**. Blend in 2 cups **milk** and add 1 **vanilla bean** (use the one the oranges cooked with, or add vanilla extract later, as directed). Bring to a boil over medium-high heat, stirring.

In a bowl, beat 4 large **egg yolks** to blend. Stir ½ cup of the hot milk mixture into yolks, then stir all back into pan. Stir over low heat for 5 minutes. Lift out vanilla bean, rinse, and let dry, then reserve to use again. (If not using bean, add ½ teaspoon vanilla.) Let cool, then cover and refrigerate for at least 3 hours or up to 2 days.

Roast Beef Dinner

(Also pictured on front cover)

This elegant dinner for 8 to 10 guests features a substantial beef roast. As a starter, offer paper-thin prosciutto slices (you'll need ½ to ⅓ lb.) with cracked pepper and a touch of olive oil. Serve up the roast with a corn "risotto" and rolls of Swiss chard; then offer a mid-meal refresher of Cabernet Sauvignon Ice. Follow with ripe Brie, toasted baguette slices, and chilled watercress tossed with your favorite light dressing. (Buy 1 to 1¼ lbs. Brie, one or two baguettes, and two or three large bunches of watercress.) For dessert, present luscious White Chocolate Baskets.

MENU

Prosciutto with Pepper & Oil
Beef Rib Roast
with Tangerine Glaze
Corn Risotto
Swiss Chard, Florentine Style
Cabernet Sauvignon Ice
Brie with Toasted Baguettes
& Watercress
White Chocolate Baskets

Beef Rib Roast with Tangerine Glaze

4   cups tangerine or
    orange juice
1   beef rib roast
    (7 to 10 lbs.)
1   pound small whole
    onions (about 1 inch in
    diameter), peeled
2   jars (8 oz. **each**)
    vacuum-packed whole
    chestnuts; or 2 cans
    (15½ oz. **each**) whole
    chestnuts in water,
    drained
    Tangerine wedges and
    rosemary sprigs
3   tablespoons orange-
    flavored liqueur

In an 8- to 10-inch frying pan, boil tangerine juice, uncovered, over high heat until reduced to about ⅔ cup; stir to prevent scorching. Set glaze aside.

Set beef, fat side up, directly in a roasting pan (at least 12 by 15 inches). Roast, uncovered, in a 325° oven until a meat thermometer inserted in thickest part (not touching bone) registers at least 130°F for rare—about 2 hours and 20 minutes for a 7-pound roast, about 3 hours and 20 minutes for a 10-pound roast (allow 20 minutes *total* per pound).

About 2 hours before roast is done, put onions in pan; 1 hour later, add chestnuts. About 10 minutes before roast is done, brush half the tangerine glaze over both meat and onions.

Transfer roast, onions, and chestnuts to a platter; let stand for about 20 minutes before carving (keep warm). Garnish with tangerine wedges and rosemary.

Skim and discard fat from pan juices, then add remaining tangerine glaze to pan juices. Bring to a boil over medium-high heat, scraping pan to loosen crusty bits. Add liqueur; pour into a serving dish. Carve meat, then spoon sauce over individual portions. Makes 8 to 10 servings.

Corn Risotto

Melt 6 tablespoons **butter** or margarine in a 10- to 12-inch frying pan over high heat. Add 1 large **onion**, finely chopped. Cook, stirring often, until onion is slightly browned.

Add 4 cups fresh or frozen **corn kernels** (you'll need 6 ears of corn or two 10-oz. packages frozen corn kernels). Then stir in 1 cup **whipping cream**. Stir over high heat until almost all liquid has boiled away; remove from heat.

Finely sliver 1 small fresh or canned **black or white truffle** (at least ½ oz.). Stir ¼ of the slivers (and liquid from canned truffle) into corn mixture; set aside remaining slivers.

Pour corn into a shallow 1½-quart baking dish. Scatter 2 cups (8 oz.) shredded **fontina cheese** over corn. Bake, uncovered, in a 400° oven until cheese is melted and slightly browned (about 10 minutes). Sprinkle remaining truffle slivers over cheese. Makes 8 to 10 servings.

Swiss Chard, Florentine Style

2   pounds green Swiss
    chard
1   tablespoon lemon juice
3   tablespoons olive oil
    Salt and freshly ground
    pepper
    Lemon wedges

Wash chard leaves well. Cut off discolored stem bases and discard, then cut off stems at base of leaves. Set stems and leaves aside separately.

In a 5- to 6-quart pan, bring 3 quarts of water to a boil. Push stems down into water. Cook, uncovered, until limp (about 4 minutes). Lift out.

At once, push leaves gently down into boiling water and cook until limp (1 to 2 minutes). Lift out carefully and drain. To preserve the best green color, immerse at once in ice water. When cool, drain.

Select 8 to 10 of the largest, most perfect leaves and set aside. Chop remaining leaves and stems together. Mix with lemon juice and 2 tablespoons of the oil. Season to taste with salt and pepper.

Lay out reserved leaves; mound an equal amount of chopped chard on each. Fold each leaf to enclose filling; set seam side down on a serving dish. If made ahead, cover and refrigerate for up to 24 hours.

To serve, drizzle with remaining oil and accompany with lemon wedges to squeeze on individual servings. Makes 8 to 10 servings.

Cabernet Sauvignon Ice

3/4   cup sugar
1   cup water
1 1/2   cups Cabernet
      Sauvignon
1 1/2   cups white grape juice
3/4   cup lemon juice
      Mint sprigs (optional)
      Red grapes (optional)

In a 1- to 1 1/2-quart pan, combine sugar, water, and wine. Bring to a boil, then reduce heat and simmer gently for 5 minutes. Remove from heat; let cool. Stir in grape juice and lemon juice; cover and refrigerate until cold (at least 1 hour).

Pour mixture into 2 or 3 divided ice cube trays or a shallow 9-inch square metal pan. Freeze until solid (about 4 hours).

If ice is frozen in a pan, let it stand at room temperature until you can break it into chunks with a spoon. Then place ice cubes or chunks, 1/3 to 1/2 at a time, in a food processor; use on-off bursts to break up ice, then process continuously until ice is a velvety slush. Or beat all the ice with an electric mixer, gradually increasing speed from low to high as ice softens.

Spoon into a container; cover and freeze until solid (or for up to 1 month). Garnish servings with mint and grapes, if desired. Makes about 5 cups (8 to 10 mid-meal servings).

White Chocolate Baskets

8   ounces white chocolate
      White Chocolate Mousse
      (recipe follows)
      Poached Cranberries
      (recipe follows)
      Thin strands of
      orange peel

Place chocolate in the top of a double boiler over simmering water. Stir

An elegant succession of courses leads diners from the smoky flavor of prosciutto to the sweetness of white chocolate in this imaginative menu. Beef rib roast with Swiss chard and corn risotto is followed by a frosty wine-flavored sorbet, then a Brie-and-salad combination. Delicate white chocolate baskets of fluffy mousse are the grand finale.

chocolate occasionally just until melted. Remove from hot water.

While chocolate is melting, grease 8 to 10 muffin cups (2 1/2-inch diameter) with solid vegetable shortening. Line each cup with a 5-inch square of plastic wrap (shortening helps hold wrap in place). Do not trim off excess plastic. Place about 1 tablespoon melted chocolate in bottom of each cup. With a small brush, paint chocolate up pan sides. Refrigerate until firm (about 1 hour) or for up to 1 week. Lift chocolate cups from pans and carefully peel off plastic; avoid touching chocolate.

Fill each chocolate basket with an equal amount of cold White Chocolate Mousse and top with a few Poached Cranberries (and some of the cranberry poaching liquid, if desired). Garnish with orange peel. To eat, scoop out mousse with a spoon, then crack chocolate basket into bite-size pieces. Makes 8 to 10 servings.

White Chocolate Mousse. Place 6 ounces **white chocolate** in the top of a double boiler over simmering water; stir occasionally until melted. In a small bowl, beat 3 large **egg whites** until foamy. Gradually beat in 1 tablespoon **sugar**, beating until stiff. Fold in hot melted chocolate until blended. In another small bowl, beat 1/2 cup **whipping cream** until stiff. Add cream to egg white mixture; fold to blend. Cover and refrigerate until cold (at least 1 hour) or until next day.

Poached Cranberries. In a 1- to 1 1/2-quart pan, combine 1/2 teaspoon grated **orange peel**, 1/4 cup **orange juice**, 2 tablespoons **sugar**, and 3/4 cup **fresh or frozen cranberries**. Simmer, uncovered, until cranberries pop (about 5 minutes). Let cool, then cover and refrigerate until cold.

Make-ahead Christmas Dinner

If Christmas Day is too hectic for lots of cooking, or if you've had your traditional holiday dinner on Christmas Eve, this make-ahead menu may be just the thing you're looking for. It's a delicious dinner for six, starring a creamy, delicate seafood manicotti that can be assembled the day before serving. You can also make the spicy, crisp-fried legumes well in advance (or just buy salted nuts). The colorful vegetable salad and rich, chocolate-crusted eggnog pie *must* be made ahead—to give the pie filling time to set and allow the salad's flavors to blend. Put together the quick and easy bacon-wrapped date appetizer the day of the party, purchase beverages and rolls—then relax and enjoy your own party!

MENU
Bacon-wrapped Dates
Legume Crisps or Salted Nuts
Apéritif of your choice
Festive Salad Bowl
Seafood Manicotti
Warm Dinner Rolls   Butter
Chocolate Swirl Eggnog Pie

Bacon-wrapped Dates

12   slices bacon
24   pitted dates

Cut each bacon slice in half crosswise. Place half-slices on a rimmed baking sheet and broil 6 inches below heat until partially cooked but still soft (about 2½ minutes). Transfer to paper towels and let drain; discard excess fat from pan.

Preheat oven to 400°. Place 1 date at end of each bacon piece and roll up; place seam side down on baking sheet. Bake until bacon is crisp and dates are heated through (about 7 minutes). Serve warm. Makes 2 dozen.

Legume Crisps

1   cup dried garbanzo beans, brown or red (decorticated, sometimes called Persian) lentils, or green or yellow split peas
3   tablespoons salad oil
     Cumin Salt, Curry Salt, Red Spices Salt (recipes follow), or coarse salt (optional)

Sort legumes and remove any debris. In a 2- to 3-quart pan, bring 4 cups water and any one of the legumes (except red lentils) to a boil over high heat. Cover and remove from heat; let stand until grains are just tender enough to chew. Allow about 15 minutes for garbanzo beans or brown lentils, about 10 minutes for green or yellow split peas.

To prepare red lentils, put in a bowl and cover with about 4 cups hottest tap water; let stand until lentils are just tender to bite (about 10 minutes).

For each legume, line a rimmed 10- by 15-inch baking pan with several layers of paper towels. Spread drained legumes out in pan and let dry for about 1 hour; blot occasionally with more paper towels.

In a 10- to 12-inch frying pan, stir legumes and oil over medium-high heat until legumes smell toasted and become dry and crisp to bite (5 to 10 minutes). Spread out on paper towels to drain; blot off excess oil with more towels.

Pour legumes into a serving bowl. Flavor with seasoned salt or coarse salt, if desired; serve immediately or store airtight for up to 2 weeks. Makes about 1½ cups.

Cumin Salt. Combine ½ teaspoon **coarse salt**, ¼ teaspoon *each* **ground cumin** and **celery salt**, and ⅛ teaspoon *each* **ground red pepper** (cayenne) and **garlic powder**.

Curry Salt. Combine 1 teaspoon **coarse salt**, ¾ teaspoon **curry powder**, and ½ teaspoon **dry mustard**.

Red Spices Salt. Combine ¾ teaspoon **coarse salt**, ½ teaspoon *each* **chili powder** and **paprika**, and ½ teaspoon **ground red pepper** (cayenne).

Festive Salad Bowl

1   pound green beans, cut diagonally into 2-inch pieces
1   can (6 to 8 oz.) water chestnuts, drained and sliced
½   pound mushrooms, sliced
1   can (8 oz.) pitted ripe olives, drained
16   to 18 cherry tomatoes, halved
2   jars (6 oz. **each**) marinated artichoke hearts
½   teaspoon dry basil
¼   teaspoon **each** dry oregano leaves and grated lemon peel
2   teaspoons lemon juice
     Garlic salt and pepper

In a 3-quart pan, bring about 1 inch of water to a boil over high heat. Add beans. When water returns to a boil, reduce heat, cover, and cook until beans are tender-crisp to bite (4 to 7 minutes). Drain and plunge immediately into cold water; when cool, drain again. Place beans in a salad bowl.

Add water chestnuts, mushrooms, olives, and tomatoes to beans. Drain artichokes, reserving marinade; add artichokes (halved, if large) to bean mixture.

In a small bowl, combine reserved marinade, basil, oregano, lemon peel, and lemon juice; stir into vegetables. Season to taste with garlic salt and pepper. Cover and refrigerate for at least 4 hours or until next day. Makes 6 to 8 servings.

Seafood Manicotti

2 tablespoons butter or margarine

1 medium-size onion, finely chopped

1 medium-size carrot, shredded

¼ cup chopped parsley

1 can (1 lb.) tomatoes

1 cup regular-strength chicken broth

1 teaspoon dry basil

¾ pound cooked fresh or canned crab, flaked

½ pound small cooked shrimp

3 green onions (including tops), thinly sliced

1 cup (4 oz.) shredded fontina cheese

6 large manicotti or other tube-shaped pasta
Fontina White Sauce (recipe follows)

½ cup grated Parmesan cheese

In a wide frying pan, melt butter over medium heat. Add onion and carrot and cook, stirring, until soft. Stir in parsley, tomatoes (break up with a spoon) and their liquid, broth, and basil. Reduce heat and simmer, uncovered, until sauce thickens (about 30 minutes). Set aside.

In a large bowl, combine crab, shrimp, green onions, and fontina cheese; set filling aside.

Cook manicotti in boiling salted water according to package directions just until tender to bite; *do not overcook.* Drain, rinse with cold water, and drain again. Meanwhile, prepare Fontina White Sauce.

Stuff each manicotti with about 5 tablespoons of the crab filling. Spoon half the tomato sauce into a shallow 3-quart casserole or 9- by 13-inch baking dish. Arrange filled pasta side by side in sauce. Pour some of the remaining sauce into casserole (but not directly over pasta). Spoon white sauce down center of manicotti and sprinkle with ⅓ cup of the Parmesan cheese. (At this point, you may cool, cover, and refrigerate until next day.)

Bake, uncovered, in a 375° oven until lightly browned and heated through (20 to 25 minutes; 35 minutes, if refrigerated). Sprinkle with remaining Parmesan cheese and offer any remaining sauce. Makes 6 servings.

Fontina White Sauce. In a wide frying pan, melt ¼ cup (⅛ lb.) **butter** or margarine over medium heat. Add 1 small **onion,** finely chopped, and cook, stirring, until soft. Blend in 2 tablespoons **all-purpose flour** and cook, stirring, until bubbly. Gradually pour in ¾ cup *each* **milk** and **regular-strength chicken broth** and cook, stirring, until sauce boils and thickens. Remove from heat.

Add 1 cup (4 oz.) shredded **fontina cheese,** 2 tablespoons **dry vermouth,** and ⅛ teaspoon *each* **ground nutmeg** and **white pepper.** Stir just until cheese is melted.

Chocolate Swirl Eggnog Pie

¼ cup cold water

1 envelope unflavored gelatin

2 tablespoons cornstarch

½ cup sugar

2 cups commercial eggnog

1½ ounces semisweet chocolate, melted

1 cup whipping cream

6 tablespoons rum or ¾ teaspoon rum flavoring
Chocolate Crust (recipe follows)
Semisweet chocolate curls

Pour water into a small bowl and sprinkle with gelatin; set aside. In a pan, stir together cornstarch, sugar, and eggnog; cook over medium heat, stirring, until thickened. Stir in softened gelatin. Divide mixture in half and stir melted chocolate into 1 portion. Refrigerate both portions until thick but not set.

In a bowl, beat cream until it holds soft peaks; fold whipped cream and rum into plain portion of filling, then spoon into cooled Chocolate Crust. Spoon chocolate portion over top. With a knife, gently swirl chocolate layer through rum layer. Refrigerate until well chilled. Sprinkle with chocolate curls before serving. Makes 8 servings.

Chocolate Crust. In a large bowl, combine 1 cup **all-purpose flour**, ¼ cup firmly packed **brown sugar**, ¾ cup finely chopped **nuts**, and 1 ounce **semisweet chocolate**, grated. Stir in ⅓ cup **butter** or margarine, melted; press mixture over bottom and sides of a 9-inch pie pan. Bake in a 375° oven for 15 minutes. Let cool.

New Year's Day Breakfast

■

On the first day of the brand-new year, wake up to this simple yet festive breakfast of cranberry scones with orange-flavored cream cheese, fruit compote, crisp bacon, and hot cocoa. You can bake the scones and bacon in the same oven.

Wonderful, juicy winter oranges star in this menu. Orange peel goes into the scones and cream cheese; the orange segments are part of the fruit compote. To make the compote, cut segments free from the membranes and mix with peeled, sliced kiwi fruit and canned sliced pears in their own juice; to serve four to six people, you'll need 4 medium-size oranges, 2 medium-size kiwi fruit, and 1 can (1 lb.) sliced pears. Spoon the fruit into champagne flutes and fill with sparkling apple cider or sparkling wine.

MENU
Cranberry-Walnut Scones
Whipped Honey-Orange
Cream Cheese
Oven-fried Bacon
Sparkling Fruit Compote
Hot Cocoa

Sweet and simple, *the perfect breakfast for New Year's Day begins with a sparkling fruit compote and then moves on to warm scones with orange-flavored whipped cream cheese and crisp bacon. Steaming hot cocoa completes the menu.*

Cranberry-Walnut Scones

3   cups all-purpose flour
½   cup sugar
1   tablespoon baking powder
½   teaspoon **each** baking soda and salt
¾   cup (⅜ lb.) butter or margarine, cut into small pieces
1   cup fresh or frozen cranberries
½   cup chopped walnuts
1½   teaspoons grated orange peel
1   cup buttermilk
    About 1 tablespoon whipping cream or milk
1   tablespoon sugar mixed with ¼ teaspoon ground cinnamon and ⅛ teaspoon ground allspice

In a large bowl, stir together flour, the ½ cup sugar, baking powder, baking soda, and salt. Using a pastry blender or your fingers, cut or rub butter into flour mixture until coarse crumbs form; stir in cranberries, walnuts, and orange peel. Add buttermilk and mix with a fork just until dough is evenly moistened.

Gather dough into a ball and place on a floured board. Roll or pat into a ¾-inch-thick circle. Using a 2½-inch-diameter cutter, cut into rounds. Place on a greased 12- by 15-inch baking sheet, spacing rounds 1½ inches apart. Reroll and cut scraps. Brush tops of scones with cream; sprinkle with sugar-spice mixture.

Bake on lowest rack of a 400° oven until tops are lightly browned (14 to 16 minutes). Serve warm. Makes 1 dozen, 4 to 6 servings.

Whipped Honey-Orange Cream Cheese

In a small bowl, beat 1 large package (8 oz.) **cream cheese** (at room temperature), 2 tablespoons **honey,** and 1 tablespoon grated **orange peel** until light and fluffy. If made ahead, cover and refrigerate for up to 2 days. Makes about 1¼ cups, 4 to 6 servings.

Oven-fried Bacon

Line a 10- by 15-inch rimmed baking pan with foil; place a wire rack over pan. Lay 12 to 14 slices **bacon** (about 1 lb.), slightly overlapping, on rack. Bake on upper rack of a 400° oven until browned and crisp (14 to 16 minutes). Serves 4 to 6.

Index

Addendum cookies, 21
Almond
    bark, 54
    Christmas wreath, cherry-, 78
    crescents, 5
    filling, cherry-, 78
    fruitcake, golden apricot-, 41
    homemade marzipan, 54
    icing, 37
    ravioli cookies, 17
    sculpture cookies, 10
    sculpture dough, cocoa-, 10
    tea loaf, eggnog, 27
    thins, spiced, 25
    toffee, 55
Anise
    bread, 35
    cookies, 16
    pretzels, 5
Appetizer pastries, savory fila, 63
Apple
    fruitcake, spiced, 41
    pie, caramel-topped, 47
Apricot
    -almond fruitcake, golden, 41
    filling, 16
    slims, 51
    spread, tangy, 29
Artichoke halves, cooked, 68

Bacon, oven-fried, 94
Bacon-wrapped dates, 92
Baked sausage with sweet red
    peppers & mushrooms, oven
    polenta &, 77
Bar cookies, 22–24
Basic cooked buttercream, 74
Beans, green, & tomatoes, savory, 71
Beef
    rib roast with tangerine glaze, 90
    roast ribs, 68
Beets, pickled, & purple eggs, 59
Belgian cramique, 37
Beverages
    New Mexican hot chocolate, 78
    praline eggnog, 76
    sparkling cranberry blush cocktail,
        76
    spiced milk, 72
Biscuits, poppy seed–herb drop, 59
Black & white squares, 26
Blond creme fudge, 50
Bohemian Christmas braid, 36
Boned turkey with rice & sausage
    stuffing, 81
Bourbon chews, 20
Brandy balls, 7
Breads, 27–39
    anise, 35
    Belgian cramique, 37
    Bohemian Christmas braid, 36
    cherry-almond Christmas wreath, 78
    Christmas surprise bread bundles,
        32
    Christmas tree, 36
    cranberry-nut bread, 29
    cut-and-slash loaves, 32
    date-nut loaf, 27
    double cheese, 65
    Dresden-style stollen, 38
    eggnog almond tea loaf, 27
    glazed lemon, 27
    golden teddy bear, 30
    mincemeat, 28
    miniature, 31
    panettone, 28
    poppy seed loaf, 29
    pumpkin, 66
    quick orange loaves, 28
    Russian krendl', 38
    Swedish kardemummakrans, 31
    Swedish letter buns (lussekätter), 37
    vanocka, 35
Bread stuffing, homemade, 70
Broccoli, mashed potatoes &, 88
Brown giblet gravy, 70
Brownies, triple-layered mint, 24

Brown sugar fudge, peanut butter–, 51
Brown sugar shortbreads, 13
Bûche de Noël, 74
Buffet party, expandable, 64–67
Buttercream, basic cooked, 74
Butter pastry, 49
Butterscotch fudge, 50
Butter wafers, French, 25
Buttery cookie brittle, 24

Cabernet Sauvignon ice, 91
Cakes, 40–43. See also Fruitcakes
    bûche de Noël, 74
    carrot, 40
    cheesecake petit fours, 43
    chocolate liqueur pound, 40
    eggnog pound, 43
    Finnish ribbon, 9
    liqueur pound, 40
    pork sausage, 67
    raisin-nut loaves, 43
    seed, 67
    spice, with caramel icing, 67
    walnut-rum torte, 75
Candies, 50–55. See also Fudge
    almond bark, 54
    almond toffee, 55
    apricot slims, 51
    chocolate toffee, 55
    chocolate truffles, 76
    coconut-date logs, 52
    creamy vanilla caramels, 50
    fruit & granola slices, 52
    fruit & nut slices, 52
    hazelnut chocolate truffles, 51
    hazelnut-topped toffee, 55
    homemade marzipan, 54
    pear slims, 51
    rocky road, 55
    sugared walnuts & pecans, 54
    walnut nuggets, 52
Candy cane crisps, 8
Caramel icing, spice cake with, 67
Caramels, creamy vanilla, 50
Caramel-topped apple pie, 47
Carrots
    cake, 40
    minted, 89
    -parsnip tart, 82
    salad, tuna-, 72
Caterpillar sandwich, 72
Chard, Swiss, Florentine style, 90
Cheese
    bread, double, 65
    cream, frosting, 41
    cream, pastry, 48
    cream, whipped honey-orange, 94
    filling, feta, 63
    filling, savory, 35
    filling, sweet, 34
    -mushroom fingers, 63
    pork loin stuffed with two, 60
    port-poached pears with Stilton
        custard, 82
    stack, shrimp, 70
    torta, layered, 62
Cheesecake petit fours, 43
Cherry-almond Christmas wreath, 78
Chestnut clouds, 77
Children's Christmas party, 72–73
Chilled leeks & shrimp, 84
Chinese plum sauce, 82
Chocolate
    creme fudge, 50
    crust, 93
    -dipped sugarplums, 72
    liqueur pound cake, 40
    New Mexican hot, 78
    rocky road, 55
    swirl eggnog pie, 93
    toffee, 55
    trifle, fresh orange &, 89
    truffles, 76
    truffles, hazelnut, 51
    white, baskets, 91
    white, mousse, 91
Choco-peanut creme fudge, 50
Christmas Eve family supper, 77
Christmas morning breakfast, 78–79
Christmas surprise bread bundles, 32
Christmas tree bread, 36
Cocoa-almond sculpture dough, 10
Coconut-date logs, 52
Colorful fruitcake loaves, 42
Colorful fruitcake rounds, 42
Cooked artichoke halves, 68

Cookies
    addendum, 21
    almond crescents, 5
    almond ravioli, 17
    almond sculpture, 10
    anise, 16
    anise pretzels, 5
    black & white squares, 26
    bourbon chews, 20
    brandy balls, 7
    brown sugar shortbreads, 13
    buttery cookie brittle, 24
    candy cane crisps, 8
    cookie canvases, 12
    crisp oatmeal fruit strips, 6
    easy-to-cut, 11
    English toffee squares, 24
    Finnish ribbon cakes, 9
    Finnish rye, 11
    French butter wafers, 25
    fruit bars, 16
    fruitcake cookie cups, 20
    gingerbread boys, 13
    gingerbread log cabin, 18
    ginger shortbread, 22
    glazed mincemeat drops, 20
    holiday date-nut drops, 21
    Nürnberger lebkuchen, 17
    nutmeg crisps, 14
    packaging & sending, 9
    persimmon bars, 22
    pine nut sugar, 13
    poppy seed nut slices, 25
    Scottish shortbread, 22
    sour cream spice, 13
    speculaas, 6
    spiced almond thins, 25
    spritz, 8
    stained-glass, 14
    sugar, 11
    Swedish ginger thins, 19
    Swedish pinwheel, 12
    thumbprint, 8
    triple-layered mint brownies, 24
    tutti frutti oat bars, 22
    twice-baked walnut, 6
Corn
    & red pepper relish salad, 59
    risotto, 90
Crab, cracked, with melted butter, 68
Cracked crab with melted butter, 68
Cramique, Belgian, 37
Cranberries
    blush cocktail, sparkling, 76
    crunch pie, 47
    mulled, 60
    -nut bread, 29
    -pepper sauce, roast pork with, 88
    poached, 91
    -walnut scones, 94
Cream, pastry, 89
Cream cheese
    frosting, 41
    pastry, 48
    whipped honey-orange, 94
Cream of pistachio soup, 88
Creamy pumpkin pie squares, 48
Creamy vanilla caramels, 50
Crisp oatmeal fruit strips, 6
Crisp persimmon pie, 47
Cumin salt, 92
Curry salt, 92
Custard, Stilton, port-poached pears
    with, 82
Cut-and-slash loaves, 32
Cutout cookies, 11–19

Dates
    bacon-wrapped, 92
    filling, 16
    logs, coconut-, 52
    -nut drops, holiday, 21
    nut loaf, 27
Dessert buffet, festive, 74–76
Dill salad, radicchio, shrimp &, 81
Dip, green goddess, shrimp with, 62
Double cheese bread, 65
Double-crust flaky pastry, 44
Dresden-style stollen, 38
Drop cookies, 20–21

Easy-going holiday suppers, 68–69
Easy-to-cut cookies, 11
Edible-pod peas, 69

Eggnog
    almond tea loaf, 27
    pie, chocolate swirl, 93
    pound cake, 43
    praline, 76
Eggplant relish, Italian, 62
Eggs, purple, pickled beets &, 59
English toffee squares, 24

Fennel & watercress salad, 89
Festive salad bowl, 92
Feta cheese filling, 63
Fig filling, 16
Fila appetizer pastries, savory, 63
Finnish ribbon cakes, 9
Finnish rye cookies, 11
Flaky pastry, 44
Flaky pastry, double-crust, 44
Fontina white sauce, 93
French butter wafers, 25
Fresh orange & chocolate trifle, 89
Frostings
    basic cooked buttercream, 74
    cream cheese, 41
Fruit
    bars, 16
    filling, 22
    & granola slices, 52
    & nut slices, 52
    port-poached, 85
    strips, crisp oatmeal, 6
Fruitcakes
    cookie cups, 20
    golden apricot-almond, 41
    loaves, colorful, 42
    rounds, colorful, 42
    spiced, apple, 41
    Western, 74
Fudge
    blond creme, 50
    butterscotch, 50
    chocolate creme, 50
    choco-peanut creme, 50
    peanut butter–brown sugar, 51
    peppermint creme, 50

Giblet
    gravy, brown, 70
    wine sauce, roast goose with, 84
Ginger
    shortbread, 22
    thins, Swedish, 19
Gingerbread
    boys, 13
    log cabin, 18
Glazed lemon bread, 27
Glazed mincemeat drops, 20
Glazes
    lemon, 23, 27
    rum, 17
    spicy, 21
    sugar, 35, 39, 78
    tangerine, beef rib roast with, 90
Golden apricot-almond fruitcake, 41
Golden teddy bear breads, 30
Goose, roast, with giblet wine sauce, 84
Granola slices, fruit &, 52
Gravy, brown giblet, 70
Green goddess dip, shrimp with, 62

Ham salad, 72
Hand-molded & pressed cookies, 5–10
Hard sauce, whipped, 45
Harvest moon squash pie, 45
Hazelnut
    chocolate truffles, 51
    -topped toffee, 55
Herb drop biscuits, poppy seed–, 59
Holiday date-nut drops, 21
Homemade bread stuffing, 70
Homemade marzipan, 54
Honey-orange cream cheese,
    whipped, 94

Ice, Cabernet Sauvignon, 91
Icebox cookies, 25–26
Icings
    almond, 37
    caramel, 67
    lemon, 31
    royal, 19
    white, 19
Italian eggplant relish, 62

Jam tart, raspberry, 61

Kardemummakrans, Swedish, 31
Krendl', Russian, 38

Lamb filling, spicy, 63
Layered cheese torta, 62
Layered yam casserole, 85
Lebkuchen, Nürnberger, 17
Leeks, chilled, & shrimp, 84
Legume crisps, 92
Lemon
    bread, glazed, 27
    glaze, 23, 27
    icing, 31
Letter buns, Swedish (lussekätter), 37
Lettuce, peas with, 82
Liqueur
    pound cake, 40
    pound cake, chocolate, 40
    syrup, 40
Log cabin, gingerbread, 18
Lussekätter (Swedish letter buns), 37

Make-ahead Christmas dinner, 92–93
Manicotti, seafood, 93
Marzipan, homemade, 54
Mashed potato casserole, 71
Mashed potatoes & broccoli, 88
Milk
    New Mexican hot chocolate, 78
    praline eggnog, 76
    spiced, 72
Mincemeat
    bread, 28
    drops, glazed, 20
    old-fashioned, 46
    tarts, 45
Mince pie, traditional, 45
Miniature breads, 31
Mint brownies, triple-layered, 24
Minted carrots, 89
Mousse, white chocolate, 91
Mulled cranberries, 60
Mushroom fingers, cheese-, 63
Mushrooms, sweet red peppers &,
    oven polenta & baked sausage
    with, 77

New Mexican hot chocolate, 78
New Year's Day breakfast, 94
Nürnberger lebkuchen, 17
Nut
    bread, cranberry-, 29
    drops, holiday date-, 21
    loaf, date-, 27
    loaves, raisin-, 43
    mosaic tart, 49
    slices, fruit &, 52
    slices, poppy seed, 25
Nutmeg crisps, 14

Oat bars, tutti frutti, 22
Oatmeal fruit strips, crisp, 6
Old-fashioned mincemeat, 46
Old-fashioned pumpkin pie, 44
Open house, holiday, 62–63
Orange
    cream cheese, whipped honey-, 94
    fresh, & chocolate trifle, 89
    loaves, quick, 28
Oven-fried bacon, 94
Oven polenta & baked sausage with
    sweet red peppers & mushrooms,
    77

Packaging & sending cookies, 9
Panettone, 28
Parsnip tart, carrot-, 82
Pastries, savory fila appetizer, 63
Pastry
    butter, 49
    cream cheese, 48
    double-crust flaky, 44
    flaky, 44
    press-in, 82
Pastry cream, 89
Peanut butter–brown sugar fudge, 51
Peanut creme fudge, choco-, 50

Pears
    pepper pie, 48
    port-poached, with Stilton custard, 82
    slims, 51
Peas
    edible-pod, 69
    with lettuce, 82
Pecans, sugared walnuts &, 54
Pepper, red, relish salad, corn &, 59
Peppermint creme fudge, 50
Pepper pie, pear, 48
Peppers, sweet red, & mushrooms,
    oven polenta & baked sausage
    with, 77
Pepper sauce, cranberry-, roast pork
    with, 88
Persimmon
    bars, 22
    pie, crisp, 47
    pudding, 87
    purée, 23
Petit fours, cheesecake, 43
Pickled beets & purple eggs, 59
Pies. See also Tarts
    caramel-topped apple, 47
    chocolate swirl eggnog, 93
    cranberry crunch, 47
    crisp persimmon, 47
    harvest moon squash, 45
    old-fashioned pumpkin, 44
    pear pepper, 48
    squares, creamy pumpkin, 48
    sweet yam, 44
    traditional mince, 45
Pine nut sugar cookies, 13
Pinwheel cookies, Swedish, 12
Pistachio soup, cream of, 88
Plum sauce, Chinese, 82
Poached cranberries, 91
Polenta, oven, & baked sausage with
    sweet red peppers & mushrooms,
    77
Poppy seed
    –herb drop biscuits, 59
    loaf, 29
    nut slices, 25
Pork
    loin stuffed with two cheeses, 60
    roast, with cranberry-pepper sauce,
    88
    sausage cake, 67
Port-poached fruit, 85
Port-poached pears with Stilton
    custard, 82
Potatoes
    balls, roasted, 69
    & broccoli, mashed, 88
    casserole, mashed, 71
Potluck supper, holiday, 70–71
Pound cake
    chocolate liqueur, 40
    eggnog, 43
    liqueur, 40
Praline eggnog, 76
Press-in pastry, 82
Pretzels, anise, 5
Prune filling, 16
Puddings
    persimmon, 87
    steamed, with zabaglione sauce, 69
Pumpkin
    bread, 66
    pie, old-fashioned, 44
    pie squares, creamy, 48
    squares, spicy frozen, 71

Quick breads, 27–29
Quick orange loaves, 28

Radicchio, shrimp & dill salad, 81
Raisin-nut loaves, 43
Raspberry jam tart, 61
Ravioli cookies, almond, 17
Red pepper relish salad, corn &, 59
Red spices salt, 92
Relish, Italian eggplant, 62
Relish salad, corn & red pepper, 59
Ribbon cakes, Finnish, 9
Rib roast, beef, with tangerine glaze, 90
Ribs, roast, 68
Rice
    salad, wild, 60
    & sausage stuffing, boned turkey
    with, 81
    stuffing, sherried wild, 57

Risotto, corn, 90
Roast beef dinner, 90–91
Roasted potato balls, 69
Roast goose dinner, 84–87
Roast goose with giblet wine sauce, 84
Roast pork dinner, 88–89
Roast pork with cranberry-pepper
    sauce, 88
Roast ribs, 68
Roast turkey dinner, 81–83
Roast turkey with all the trimmings, 57
Rocky road, 55
Royal icing, 19
Rum
    glaze, 17
    torte, walnut-, 75
Russian krendl', 38
Rye cookies, Finnish, 11

Salads
    bowl, festive, 92
    corn & red pepper relish, 59
    fennel & watercress, 89
    ham, 72
    radicchio, shrimp & dill, 81
    Sicilian green, 77
    tuna-carrot, 72
    wild rice, 60
Salts
    cumin, 92
    curry, 92
    red spices, 92
Sandwich, caterpillar, 72
Sauces
    Chinese plum, 82
    cranberry-pepper, roast pork with,
    88
    fontina white, 93
    giblet wine, roast goose with, 84
    soft, 87
    whipped hard, 45
    zabaglione, steamed pudding with,
    69
Sausage
    baked, oven polenta &, with sweet
    red peppers & mushrooms, 77
    pork, cake, 67
    soup, green bean &, 77
    stuffing, rice &, boned turkey with,
    81
Savory cheese filling, 35
Savory fila appetizer pastries, 63
Savory green beans & tomatoes, 71
Scones, cranberry-walnut, 94
Scottish shortbread, 22
Sculpture cookies, almond, 10
Seafood manicotti, 93
Seed cake, 67
Sherried wild rice stuffing, 57
Shortbreads
    brown sugar, 13
    ginger, 22
    Scottish, 22
Shrimp
    cheese stack, 70
    chilled leeks &, 84
    & dill salad, radicchio, 81
    with green goddess dip, 62
Sicilian green salad, 77
Soft sauce, 87
Soups
    cream of pistachio, 88
    green bean & sausage, 77
Sour cream spice cookies, 13
Sour cream topping, 49
Sparkling cranberry blush cocktail, 76
Speculaas, 6
Spice cake with caramel icing, 67
Spice cookies, sour cream, 13
Spiced almond thins, 25
Spiced apple fruitcake, 41
Spiced milk, 72
Spice mixture, 82
Spicy frozen pumpkin squares, 71
Spicy glaze, 21
Spicy lamb filling, 63
Spinach-stuffed tomatoes, 87
Spritz, 8
Squash, baked, 45
Squash pie, harvest moon, 45
Stained-glass cookies, 14
Steamed pudding with zabaglione
    sauce, 69
Stilton custard, port-poached pears
    with, 82
Stollen, Dresden-style, 38

Streusel, walnut, 48
Stuffings
    homemade bread, 70
    on the outside, turkey with, 70
    rice & sausage, boned turkey with,
    81
    sherried wild rice, 57
Sugar
    cookies, 11
    cookies, easy-to-cut, 11
    cookies, pine nut, 13
    glaze, 35, 39, 78
Sugared walnuts & pecans, 54
Sugarplums, chocolate-dipped, 72
Sun-dried tomato topping & filling, 63
Swedish ginger thins, 19
Swedish kardemummakrans, 31
Swedish letter buns (lussekätter), 37
Swedish pinwheel cookies, 12
Sweet cheese filling, 34
Sweet yam pie, 44
Swiss chard, Florentine style, 90
Syrup, liqueur, 40

Tangerine glaze, beef rib roast with, 90
Tangy apricot spread, 29
Tarts
    carrot-parsnip, 82
    mincemeat, 45
    nut mosaic, 49
    raspberry jam, 61
Teddy bear breads, golden, 30
Thanksgiving banquet, easy, 57–58
Thumbprint cookies, 8
Toffee
    almond, 55
    chocolate, 55
    hazelnut-topped, 55
    squares, English, 24
Tomatoes
    savory green beans &, 71
    spinach-stuffed, 87
    sun-dried, topping & filling, 63
Torta, layered cheese, 62
Torte, walnut-rum, 75
Traditional mince pie, 45
Tree-cutters' tailgate picnic, 59
Tree-trimmers' buffet supper, 60–61
Trifle, fresh orange & chocolate, 89
Triple-layered mint brownies, 24
Truffles
    chocolate, 76
    hazelnut chocolate, 51
Tuna-carrot salad, 72
Turkey
    boned, with rice & sausage stuffing,
    81
    roast, with all the trimmings, 57
    with stuffing on the outside, 70
Tutti frutti oat bars, 22
Twice-baked walnut cookies, 6

Vanilla caramels, creamy, 50
Vanocka, 35

Walnuts
    cookies, twice-baked, 6
    nuggets, 52
    & pecans, sugared, 54
    -rum torte, 75
    scones, cranberry-, 94
    streusel, 48
Watercress salad, fennel &, 89
Western fruitcake, 74
Whipped honey-orange cream
    cheese, 94
White chocolate
    baskets, 91
    mousse, 91
White icing, 19
Wild rice
    salad, 60
    stuffing, sherried, 57
Wine sauce, giblet, roast goose with,
    84

Yam casserole, layered, 85
Yam pie, sweet, 44
Yeast breads, 30–39
Yule log (bûche de Noël), 74

Zabaglione sauce, steamed pudding
    with, 69